Spiritual
WRITING

Spiritual
WRITING

From Inspiration to Publication

Deborah Levine Herman

with

Cynthia Black

BEYOND
WORDS
Publishing
I   N   C

Beyond Words Publishing, Inc.
20827 N.W. Cornell Road, Suite 500
Hillsboro, Oregon 97124-9808
503-531-8700
1-800-284-9673
www.beyondword.com
info@beyondword.com

The publisher and author gratefully acknowledge and thank Hal Zina Bennett for permission to reprint his article "Visionary Fiction: Rediscovering Ancient Paths to Truth." Copyright © 1999 by Hal Zina Bennett. Reprinted with permission.

Editors: Laura Carlsmith and Jenefer Angell
Managing editor: Julie Steigerwaldt
Proofreader: Marvin Moore
Cover art: Susan Gross
Cover design: Lisa Harrison Soltes
Interior design: Dorral Lukas
Composition: William H. Brunson Typography Services

Printed in the United States of America

Distributed to the book trade by Publishers Group West

Library of Congress Cataloging-in-Publication Data
Herman, Deborah, 1958–
    Spiritual writing : from inspiration to publication / Deborah Levine
    Herman with Cynthia Black.
        p.   cm.
    Includes bibliographical references and index.
    ISBN 1-58270-066-4 (pbk.)
    1. Religious literature—Authorship.   I. Title.
BR44 .H465   2002
808'.0662—dc21

                                                    2002037465

The corporate mission of Beyond Words Publishing, Inc.:
Inspire to Integrity

*To all those writers who are awakened
by a Divine voice and who have the
courage to heed the call*

CONTENTS

ACKNOWLEDGMENTS

There are so many special people who have contributed their love and their spirit to the journey I have taken as a writer and as a traveler on the path. My husband, Jeff, and my three children, Shana, Joshua, and Jessica, who are the loves of my life, have taught me more than they can imagine. My father, Stuart, a'va Sholom, is lovingly remembered for always cheering me on and for teaching me about business in spite of myself. My mother, Paula, is an inspiration to me for her strength, faith, and lovingness. My sister, Brenda, and my brother, Larry, have supported me in joy and sorrow, have given me good advice, and have filled me with a laughter borne of the secret language between siblings. I want to acknowledge my sisters on the journey, Dawn Christy and Rebecca Briggs, for being the most loyal and loving friends a woman can have. I also want to acknowledge Michael DeSisto, Louise Pritchett, and her son Marcus for helping me on my path toward self-awareness.

The Maui Writers Conference is a place where spiritual seeds are planted. Thanks to John and Shannon Tullius for creating such a special gathering in an enchanted land and for allowing me to be a part of it. I want to thank Jillian Manus for suggesting I turn my workshop proposal into a book and for introducing me to Cynthia Black and Richard Cohn, my publishers at Beyond Words. I also want to thank Roger Jellinek, editorial director of Inner Ocean Publishing and an organizer of the Maui Writers Conference, for giving me the chance to bring the material in this book to its first audience.

A special thank you goes to all the "spirit-friendly" editors and agents who have taken the time to contribute to this book and who are doing their part to help all of us to fulfill our journey. And thank you also to Hal Zina Bennett and David Ulrich for graciously allowing me to reprint their respective pieces in my book.

Finally, I can't possibly thank the staff of Beyond Words enough for making this book happen. In many ways it was a true collaboration. Developmental editor Laura Carlsmith, editor Jenefer Angell, and managing editor Julie Steigerwaldt each brought their skills into the mix and taught me many things. Thank you to Richard Cohn for his support, and a special thank you to Cynthia Black for her guidance and savvy and for becoming a friend.

Deborah Levine Herman

FOREWORD

As a publisher whose mission is to publish books that inspire readers to integrity, I was so pleased when Deborah Herman approached me one year at the Maui Writers Conference with her vision for this book. Spiritual writers, she felt, are a wonderfully special type of writer, people for whom the spiritual path has coincided with the self-discovery and revelations that writing can bring. She knew, however, as do I, that despite their talent and desire, many spiritual writers do not know how to translate their message into a publishable format. Even those who do understand how to create a marketable book proposal may still find it difficult to define the universality of their own spiritual experience and to express it in a way that is accessible to others.

I've been approached many times over the years to speak and consult at writing and publishing conferences on the topic of getting published. I have always enjoyed sharing my experience and publishing advice with authors and encouraging them to create a product that is both true to their souls while still conforming to the protocols of the publishing industry. But I had never thought of trying to reach more than one group at a time. The solution, Debbie explained, would be the book you now hold in your hands, one that addresses writing about the twin aspects of spiritual and highly personal topics—specifically, the unique path a person travels in unraveling life's mysteries and then the translation of those mysteries into a manuscript that is both marketable and meaningful.

Of course! Why hadn't anyone ever thought of this before? I know there are many "how to get published" books on the market. Some deal specifically with fiction, some with romance, others with poetry. But none deal with the unique and wonderful path to publication that a spiritual writer can take.

The spiritual writer's message is intensely personal to himself and his own experience. It is a message that is often difficult to translate and clearly share with others. I have seen thousands of manuscripts, many of which contain that kernel of universal wisdom which shines like a diamond but which, unfortunately, are far too "rough" overall for publication. These manuscripts are the hardest to reject. Clearly the authors have incredible insights and experiences, but without having learned how to present them in a marketable format, they can go no further than my rejection box. That is why I am so happy, with this book, to offer a tool to those writers whose only lack is their knowledge of the publishing industry and its specific requirements of writers.

As a publisher, my goal has always been to collaborate with first-time authors whose writing can indeed inspire others to integrity. To me, there is no greater joy than witnessing the culmination of an author's spiritual path: the moment he or she finally holds the published book, knowing that the hard-won wisdom within and the blood, sweat, and tears it took to write it down have been distilled into words that can reach thousands of people.

It is not an easy path. But it's one that can be demystified and made more accessible to all spiritual writers, both those with a fully developed credo and message and those who are still searching and evolving. That is why I am delighted to share with you the insights and very specific advice that are contained in this book, *Spiritual Writing: From Inspiration to Publication*. It gives you the tools you need to take your message from the heart to the printed page.

Cynthia Black

INTRODUCTION

As an agent, I have seen more book ideas, proposals, and manuscripts than I can possibly count. A large percentage of those have been about spiritual subjects, including religion, general spirituality, memoir, psychic experiences, channeling, angel communication, and direct prophecy.

But agents and publishers reject over 95 percent of the submissions they receive—spiritual or otherwise. You, as an aspiring spiritual writer, have to find a way to increase your odds of being within the 5 percent who are not only called but who are chosen.

In this book, I intend to give you both the inspiration to write and the tools you need to maneuver through the business of book publishing. The four parts in this book, "The Spiritual Writer and the Writer's Path," "From Inspiration to Manuscript," "From Manuscript to Publication," and "Spirit-Friendly Resources," are meant to guide and inform you on your journey to publication.

As a spiritual writer myself, I am with you every step of the way. Whether you classify yourself as a mystic, an evangelical Christian, or a nonreligious seeker of universal spiritual truths, you, like all spiritual writers, are somewhere along the continuum of the spiritual experience. As spiritual writers, we have been blessed with a connection to the source of all creation. We continuously examine the nature of reality. Our writing is our access to the universal database.

Part one, "The Spiritual Writer and the Writer's Path," analyzes how the spiritual path is inextricably linked with the writer's journey. The spiritual path transcends our intellect. We can't simply check off a list of spiritual life lessons and presume that we have become enlightened. Our lessons come in ways we can't anticipate. Maybe we don't even realize when we have progressed, but our progress is nonetheless noted, and if we figure out that there is an overall plan for our individual soul's growth, we can become active participants.

There are specific lessons that we all encounter, which I call the "seven lessons" of the spiritual path. Through journal exercises, I invite you to explore these lessons to create your own cosmic curriculum. The lessons can become a starting point for you on your sacred journey.

Part two, "From Inspiration to Manuscript," talks about craft and the creation of your message. Spiritual writers are sometimes so filled with joy and bliss that we want to persuade everyone to see and adopt our point of view. We are well-meaning and believe we are helping others become enlightened, but we run the risk of becoming "God-intoxicated," which will usually interfere with our objective of getting published. In this section, you'll learn how important it is to take a step back so you can present your material in a marketable way that also connects with the reader's desire to learn something about her own life. For a spiritual writer, objectivity is crucial. Even with fervor and passion, you are not going to save the world; however, through well-crafted writing, you can influence the consciousness of those people who read your words, and this is a wonderful contribution.

In part three, "From Manuscript to Publication," Cynthia Black has added her expertise from the publisher's perspective to mine as an author and agent. You will learn the players and the protocols of publishing so you do not make the easily avoided mistakes that would take your manuscript out of consideration. We'll look at two documents that can open doors: the query letter and the book proposal. The book proposal is an art form, and creating one that stands out will increase your credibility tremendously and move your book to the top of the submissions pile. In this publishing primer, you will also learn what happens after you get an offer from either an agent or a publisher and about your role in book marketing and promotion.

The reality of the book business is that publishers are constrained by the bottom line. Most publishing houses look for books that can fit within the mainstream, because that's where they can reach the widest audiences possible. So, what if you are a New Age or Christian writer? Is there a market for you? You bet! It's smaller than the mainstream market, but it is out there. Quite a number of publishers pride themselves on their unique niche. Your special task is to find them. They are waiting for you!

Part four, "Spirit-Friendly Resources," directs you to publishers and agents who are receptive to spiritual material. As you will learn, you increase your chances tremendously if you get your submission to the right person at the right publishing house. Conversely, you are simply wasting your time and money if you target publishers who indicate no interest in the material you are trying to present. Not all books belong at the large New York publishing houses, most of which are more constrained by the need to publish mainstream material than are the smaller firms. Large houses are less willing to take chances on new topics or new writers.

There are a hundred nuances in the spiritual-book genre. A smart writer won't waste time sending a New Age manuscript to a Christian publisher. And a writer whose work reflects his strong traditional religious beliefs won't send a manuscript to a house that publishes alternative takes on spirituality. Submitted to the wrong house, even the most worthy manuscript will merit nothing more than a quick glance and a toss into the reject pile. The resources includes names of editors who have stated an interest in a specific type of spiritual or religious material. (But it's always best to call the houses you're interested in to verify the names and titles of every editor to whom you are submitting your query or proposal.)

The spirit within motivates spiritual writers. But if you want your book to reach the greatest possible audience, spirit is not enough: you are going to have to become a student of the market. This does not violate the essence of your spirituality. You could live isolated on a mountaintop, but the greater challenge is to live spiritually in the physical world. So be proud of the challenge you have willingly embraced. It is a privilege to share the walk with you on the path from journey to sale.

Lastly, watch for the pothole on the spiritual path called "ego." Spiritual ego will compel some writers to write because they want to *be* the message and not serve as a conduit for higher truth. The universe will weed these writers out in its own way, but it is important, as a sincere spiritual writer, to continuously check your own motives. You may have a great deal to offer, but this most difficult of all human vices, ego, may stand in your way. Hopefully, this revelation and the information in this book will keep you grounded and actively involved in your path and career choices. If you examine your life and choose to grow, you can't go wrong. You will always be given the guidance you need, even when you least expect it.

A Word about Terminology

I do not assume that spirituality necessarily has anything to do with being brought up in or adhering to a certain religion. I believe that each person needs to follow her own path, but too many efforts at being all things to all people can drive a writer to distraction.

So while I heartily respect and admire anyone's choice to know the God of their understanding, I prefer to be more generic. I am comfortable with the use of the term *God* as all-encompassing. I am also comfortable with referring to God as a male even though I acknowledge that this concept is limiting. Within these pages you will also find references to spirit, the universe, the creator, and similarly nonspecific descriptions of what might be considered, by some consensus, to be the source of divine creativity.

Deborah Levine Herman

Part One
THE SPIRITUAL WRITER
AND THE WRITER'S PATH

1

THE SPIRITUAL WRITER

The calling to write can be a blessing or the bane of your existence. Some of us are driven to write as if we were on a life-or-death mission, and others of us write as easily and as naturally as we breathe. Some of us have no idea why or how we have followed this path. There are certainly easier ways to make a living, many other careers that do not require masochism or guarantee rejection.

I have often thought that medical science should recognize a common mental disorder called "writerphrenia"—the obsessive need to remove oneself from reality and human connection for hours at a time. It is characterized by coffee drinking, snacking, hair twisting, hand wringing, and postal paranoia. I have seen people—OK, I admit it was me—who actually pray and hold ceremonies over manuscripts before placing them in the hands of the U.S. Postal Service.

While writing is a difficult path, the spiritual writer's journey is always one of rewarding transformation. While the writer shares insight and wisdom with others, the act of writing returns this wisdom to the writer, touching him with an inner light—the source of all creation. The spiritual writer accesses the inner voice that gives expression to the spirit.

The Spiritual Path

Your journey as a writer parallels your spiritual path. While the idea of a spiritual path might conjure images of peaceful meditation, wind chimes, gospel choirs, and undying faith, surely you have discovered that the spiritual path is not always serene. The process of developing awareness, serenity, and faith is often painful. Our lives are thrown into turmoil as we struggle to understand our place in the universe. Sometimes we don't have any faith at all. If our feelings are too strong or our lives too difficult, we sometimes have to detach from the process altogether until we have the strength to continue exploring.

As human beings, we are on an endless search for our identity. We learn by experience and we grow through struggle, but even knowing this we may not always be ready for the challenges as they come to us. Choosing to write, for example, can have many unexpected consequences. When you commit to this way of life, no matter what particular road you take, you may feel that your troubles are worse than before.

So what keeps you coming back for more? Perhaps you sense that there is a reason for everything and you feel a need to find out what that reason is and where it will lead you. Living on earth is in itself a spiritual path. Our entire reason for being born is to figure this out; we are students in a perpetual classroom, and everything we experience is part of our spiritual education. You can participate in a fad or live in a culture, but you can only be drawn to the spiritual path by something inside of your soul. Like a pilot light waiting for a match, your path begins long before the flame is ignited.

Why We Write

For some, the process of spiritual writing is an end in itself. While you are sharing your insight and wisdom with others through the act of writing, your wisdom increases many times over, almost as though you are being taught by your own hand. If you have a calling to write, if there is an inner voice begging to be heard, you are already blessed. Writing can be a direct link to God and to your higher self. There is no better means through which you will be able to grow and enrich your soul. You may not believe it now, but no matter how hard you try, even with all the information and tips you will read in the following chapters, you might not reach your goal of a published book. But your goal of being published may not be your true destiny. The spiritual path has many mysteries. As you may have discovered before, sometimes it's best to go along for the ride and to have faith in what unfolds.

A common thread in the submissions we have received is the sense that the writer has figured out some profound truth. This discovery is the essence of "Aha!"—the moment when the spirit and intellect collide and form a union of consciousness. Understandably, when a person decodes some of the hidden language of reality, she feels compelled to share it with others. We are all teachers by nature. When your pilot is lit and your flame bursts forth, you can become engulfed—so caught up in the ecstatic experience of awakening that you can lose your grounding. This can be a vulnerable time for those of us on the spiritual path because it is the time when we can be too anxious to share what we have learned. We run the risk of distracting ourselves and losing our discernment. We can also forget that we are not only teachers; we will *always* be students. We never teach anything that we have not needed to learn or are not still learning ourselves. Sometimes we want to share our understanding before it is fully developed and rush into trying to get it published. "Physician, heal thyself" is a good motto for the spiritual writer. Some say that each of us writes the book that *we* need to read!

You will see more clearly what this need for discernment means as you read through the chapters of this book. For example, while you want to present yourself as a person qualified to write on a spiritual subject, if you proclaim yourself the only and final authority about it, you will probably ruin your chances of being published. You will also do a disservice to your truth and the essence of your message. The key is to write with authority but not from a place of infallibility. Pilgrims on a spiritual path often find that all truth comes from the same source and that no one human being has a corner on it.

You Are Not Just a Conduit

When you are truly in the flow of writing, have you ever had the sense that you do not know where this energy comes from? Do you feel as if it is channeled from some source outside of you? But you are not a simple conduit—*you* are important to the process. This writing comes from you and your connection to God working hand in hand. You make the choice to be a vessel for this information.

You may have reached the point on your path where your writing seems effortless. For those of you who aren't there yet, take heart. You may not believe it now, but spiritual writing can be effortless if you continue to develop spiritually, follow your path, and surrender to faith. The less resistance you have, the more empowered you become, because you can draw on the resources of the universe around you. You can learn to let go. You can reach inside for this link and let its inspiration spill out. It doesn't mean you won't have to go back and edit, but the initial process can be filled with joy.

The seven spiritual lessons highlighted in chapter 3 and the progress of your soul on your spiritual path form the foundation of the message that you ultimately present for publication. As you develop in your lessons, you develop in your writing. As your writing develops and your link to God becomes stronger, you are moving forward. If you already feel clear about what you are writing and believe you are ready to share it with the world, move ahead into part two, "From Inspiration to Manuscript."

When you are finally ready to send your message out into the world, have confidence in your work. Although the spiritual path is never-ending, there is a point when you will choose to move your writing to the next step. Keep in mind that you may not succeed right away.

If not, review the advice in this book, look objectively at your work, show it to others, and keep writing!

Remember, the universe's time and our time are two entirely different things. You may feel urgency about your work, but you cannot control the realities of the publishing world. The best you can do is to learn all you can to maximize your chances of breaking through the ordinary obstacles that await you on the road to publication. Your book does not need to be published by a certain date to fulfill your mission. Too many spiritual writers are concerned that they could be messing up some divine plan if their work is not published immediately. Remember that you aren't the one in control of the divine plan. Be sure you aren't confusing the urgency to publish with the urgency your soul feels to move ahead on your path. Have faith. We are beacons, and our power and contribution are to bring more faith, love, light, and hope into the world. For this task, timing is infinite.

The universe is abundant, but we have to be realistic and responsible. In the world of spirit, anything is possible. In the physical world, nothing is achieved without a lot of roll-up-the-sleeves hard work. The writer's journey toward a sale is filled with many challenges. But you have the same chances as anyone else who is willing to do the work. Follow the advice in this book and set a clear intention. Be objective and take the time to put together your project in the most professional manner possible. If you balance your sense of mission with your knowledge of the publishing industry and your own intentions, you will greatly increase your chances for success.

2

CHALLENGES FOR THE SPIRITUAL WRITER

All spiritual disciplines are experiencing a renaissance, making this is a wonderful time to be a writer in this genre. The publishing industry, once dismissive of New Age or religious work, is now recognizing spiritual awakening as something more than a passing fad. If you are able to develop your craft, your voice, and your credibility, you could have an amazing career ahead of you!

The journey can be challenging. Most writers will encounter some significant barriers on the road to finding their most natural and comfortable writing style. And there is more to a spiritual style than the words on paper. The life of a spiritual writer does not begin, or end, with the book you publish. In this chapter we will look at some of the special challenges for a person whose spiritual path and writer's journey are one and the same.

Spiritual Writer's Block

I once had a conversation with one of my favorite Chassidic rabbis. Chassidic rabbis are strictly orthodox with long beards and a belief in the more mystical aspects of Judaism. Rabbis are respected in my home, particularly because we are not strict observers and feel humbled by their faith. When my children found out the rabbi was on his way, they ran around the house, actually cleaning—a miracle in itself—and saying "The rabbi is coming, the rabbi is coming!"

The rabbi knows I am a writer, and during our conversation about my son's Bar Mitzvah, he asked me for advice: "I am having trouble with an article I am writing. It is for the Jewish newspaper. It takes me hours to write two paragraphs and then I hate them anyway."

I was surprised that this knowledgeable and respected teacher was stumped on the same issue that I face every time I sit down to write. However, considering how many drafts I have written for my own books, I could understand his angst. At least he was asking me something in my territory. I said, "Rabbi, I think I know what the problem is."

He looked at me expectantly with those all-knowing rabbi eyes as I continued: "You have so much faith in God, and believe so strongly that anything you teach is as an emissary of God, that you feel unable to write well enough to do it justice. In other words, you try too hard."

He paused for a few minutes and pondered my words, pulling on the untrimmed ends of his beard in a gesture characteristic of great thinkers. "I believe you are right, Deborah," he replied.

"Phew," I thought. I figured I was on a roll, so I continued: "Any spiritual writer is going to feel this way. We are our own worst critics because we have so much respect for God's authority. But language is by its nature a limited medium. God has no limitations, but we have to work with what we have. If we examine every word as we write it, we will never complete anything. All we will have is a string of perfect words with no heart."

"So maybe I should write from the heart first and go back and fix it later," he said. I should have known he would catch on quickly.

"Exactly," I replied. "You are a wonderful speaker because you are confident when you have an immediate connection with your students. If you believe that you have spoken unclearly, you can correct yourself immediately. You have an element of control. When you write, you are sending your words off into the world and have to trust that they will reach the right people and will be understood. There is no immediate connection with your audience. You don't see their response and can only wonder about it."

"Or worry about it," he laughed. " I can hardly watch anyone reading something I have written. I feel like they are scrutinizing every word."

"If you write from your heart you don't have to worry about how it will be read. You can fix it mechanically, as any good editor can do, but you will know that the essence of what you have to say has been captured. When writing spiritually, it is the spirit that is important."

"Then I can get something written instead of taking hours to write two paragraphs that are going to wind up in the wastebasket anyway."

"You have a lot of important things to say that inspire people," I said. "You just need to relax about it a little."

I can't imagine the rabbi relaxing, but the lesson is true nonetheless. Trying too hard to reflect the awesome nature of what we write about can paralyze us and make us unable to write at all. As messengers, it is good to have a healthy respect for what we are writing, but we need to understand the limitations of communication. Spiritual writing is like a relay race: you hand the baton to another runner who hands it off to someone else. If you wait too long for the words to be just so, you stop the flow of activity necessary to make the team successful.

Many writers hesitate because they are afraid of not being good enough. Don't let that be you. Remember, you have a message to share, from your own unique perspective. If you feel compelled to write, assume that you have the ability. If you are able to get your fears out of the way and tap into the divine, you will have no reason to think otherwise.

Writing nonfiction is as creative a process as fiction-writing, but it is dependent on the sharing of factual information. Because we not only affect how people feel but also influence what they know, we have a responsibility to be vigilant about the accuracy of what we convey. Spiritual writing is not science, however. We do not typically have statistical data to back up our anecdotal evidence that something does or does not exist. We must often rely on observation or opinion, writing from faith and from belief. Religious writers can refer to scriptural references for examples and support. Spiritual writers may not have even this kind of tangible information to bolster their messages.

Grounding Yourself

As spiritual people, some of us risk becoming ungrounded, like hot-air balloons without a tether. When we taste the divine, it can be beyond description. Of course we then set out to describe and share our experience. But once we become aware of our spiritual mission, we need to realize that we are not the only one with an assignment. Naturally, the spiritual experience is different for everyone. But I have seen writers, including myself, become so caught up in our own experience that we write about it in a form of spirit-babble. If we want to share our experiences with others, it's important that we make them relevant and understandable to the reader.

Much of what we do here on earth is to learn to relate, not to spirit, but to our physical reality. When we place too much importance on our spirituality, we forget that we have to set real-world priorities. If we are able to ground ourselves, we can write in a way that can resonate with people who are not necessarily on our spiritual frequency. One strategy for accomplishing this is learning to tether yourself to the real world and to recognize the importance of day-to-day activities as a means of grounding. Here are a few tips to staying grounded:

- *Stay financially solvent.* Many of us would rather not deal with budgets and other such annoying details of life.

- *Plan for your goals* without waiting for fate to take over. We want to flow with spirit, but we do not want to float with no direction.
- *Engage in activities that require focus and concentration.* The simple act of washing dishes helps tether us. I am not insinuating that spiritual people are messy, but I know I can spend days lost in creative thought without realizing that I am wading in a sea of dust and clutter.
- *Engage in physical activities*, such as gardening. You and everyone else know that exercise is important to your health, but I, for one, find every excuse not to do it. Don't add guilt to your agenda. It doesn't matter what you do. If you do something physical it will help you avoid living only in your mind.
- *Care for animals.* Dogs and cats are loving and healing companions, but they also require that you take care of them. They do not grow out of the need to be fed and walked. You can also have them neutered and spayed. I bought myself a sweet trail horse. I keep him boarded at a local farm. It has been the most grounding thing I have ever done. When I take care of him or ride, I am focused on physical reality. If I don't concentrate, I am liable to be stepped on or thrown, and it wouldn't be the horse's fault, it would be mine.
- *Involve yourself in relationships with real people.* You can live a monastic life if you believe that it will bring you closer to God. However, it doesn't make sense that God would put us here with all these people if we weren't somehow supposed to learn to relate to them. Don't use your spirituality as a means of isolation. Rather, allow yourself to share the love to bring balance into your personal relationships.
- *Refocus your attention.* Stop everything, breathe, take notice of the here and now.

These are just a few of so many possible ways to stay balanced. Naturally, you will want to look to your own life and find what works best for you.

Another strategy for staying accessible to readers in the "real" world is to develop the mental discipline to write in a focused manner that can be understood by the uninitiated.

- *Outline.* When you write, strive for clarity and connection. As spiritual writers we may think we can write without any boundaries. Letting words flow is important, but structure is imperative. Outlines are your friends. They are necessary and are the best way to establish mental discipline for your writing. (For more on outlines, refer to chapter 6.)

- *Edit.* While you do not want to withhold your best writing, you do want to make sure you are not writing so far above the average reader's head that only you understand what you are talking about. As you edit, keep in mind that someone is going to be reading what you have written. People are at all levels of spiritual awareness. If you trust spirit, there will be enough in your work to meet the needs of all kinds of seekers. Make sure the language is clear and well organized. Make it user-friendly. Don't try too hard to impress or educate. In many ways, try to keep yourself out of it. It is not easy to do, but it is what writing is really all about. Even if you are writing a memoir, look at yourself as if you were a different person and observe how you appear in the pages of your manuscript. Create distance and then imbue your "character" with the feelings and characteristics that will breathe life into it. Writing that is too personal and egocentric will prevent a reader from becoming involved. Leave room for your reader to have his own thoughts, feelings, and interpretations. (For more on editing, refer to chapter 7.)

To summarize: Remember your audience, the world around you, and how you fit within the mainstream. If your message is too far away from everyone, you can be sure that few people will be "ready" for it. I have heard many editors lament that the spiritual material they receive is unfocused, esoteric, or too "out there"—and these comments come from spirit-friendly editors who *want* to find quality spiritual manuscripts. They would like nothing more than for you to become focused in your writing so they can acquire your manuscript and be able to fulfill the growing need for quality spiritual material.

Setting Your Intention

Be clear about what it is you want from your writing. Do you want it simply to help you reflect and deepen your understanding of life and its happenings? Do you want to publish your words so that they are out there for whoever can find value in them? Or do you want nothing less than a blockbuster? It's important to be clear about this, because when you set an intention, events are put in motion.

Worry and self-doubt can easily get in the way of the spiritual writer achieving the results he desires. If these become your focus, you may actually cancel out your original intent. The result? Your fears, not your goals, will be realized.

So be clear about your objectives. You're a writer, so write down your plan—and be specific. For example, "I will be published by an independent publisher and will hold two seminars each month to enhance the sales of my book." Write your goal every day if that's what it takes to keep it in the forefront of your mind.

The preceding example reflects an end goal. How about the many steps it takes to get there? They won't just happen without your conscious intent. That's where this book comes in. After you read it and learn what it takes to get published, make a monthly plan of intentions and actions leading to your final desired result. Work with devoted determination to your goal of the month. Then let go. Let the universe and its helpers arrange the details. Get out of the way!

Educating Yourself about the Publishing Experience

Setting your intention is certainly important, but setting a far-reaching goal too early in your writing career is not unlike a six-year-old who says, "I'm going to be a doctor when I grow up." She may very well be a doctor twenty years later, but she just as easily may, as she learns more about the process, decide that being a doctor is most definitely what she does *not* want. What changed? What she learned about the process was enough to cause her to form a different intention.

As an aspiring published writer, you too need to educate yourself to ensure that your intention is what you *really* want it to be. For example, you may want to be published by a large New York house in order to reach the greatest audience possible. That's a great goal, but do you know what it entails for you? Signing with a publisher is not unlike marriage: the relationship goes on and on! So learn what kind of treatment you'll get at a large house; specifically, what size print run, advance, royalties, publicity, and so on you can expect as a first-time author. Once you get this information, you may feel even more confident that this is the path for you, or you may decide to try another publishing venue.

So how, as a publishing freshman, do you learn enough to have an educated intention? Easy: You talk to people. Go to every book-signing you can and talk to the authors. Ask them about their publishing experience: Are they happy with the process? Is their relationship with their publisher what they expected? What has been the most rewarding aspect of their relationship with their publisher? What has been the most challenging? You get the idea. Writers' conferences are another way to learn about the industry so that you can set an informed intention.

Writing a Saleable Book

The Odds

The chances of your being published as a first-time author are not great. Even those spiritual writers with publishing histories can expect to have to jump through the publishing hoops each time they submit a new book. Carl McColman, buyer for New Leaf Distributing—one of the world's largest wholesale sources for all spiritual, New Age, metaphysical, occult, and world-tradition books—buys approximately four thousand titles each year from publishers, distributors, and self-publishers.

According to *The Rest of Us: The First Study of America's 53,000 Independent Smaller Book Publishers* (Book Industry Study Group, Inc., 1999), the average number of spiritual titles published per year ranged from two (for newer houses) to thirteen (for established houses, usually over ten years old). Approximately fifty thousand new books are published each year in the United States. If you consider that a large portion of these books are fiction and that nonfiction books include reference, cookbooks, art, business, collectibles, politics, diet, erotica, self-help, music, legal, history, relationships, sports, humor—you get the idea; there isn't a lot of room left for spiritual books.

I know an editor at a small imprint of a large company that receives ten thousand submissions each year. Between the four editors acquiring material, they publish sixty titles each year, and of these maybe one or two are by first-time authors. Another small spirit-friendly publishing house receives approximately three thousand unsolicited submissions each year, all of which are reviewed by only two acquisitions editors, and publishes perhaps twenty titles each year, of which only four or five may be by first-time authors.

My agency receives from fifty to one hundred submissions each week from writers seeking representation, of which we accept about 1 percent. We sell most of the books we agree to represent because we are highly selective. Note that less-discerning agencies might agree to represent a higher percentage of submissions but also may not sell everything.

So, while there are innumerable spiritual books submitted for publication each year, clearly only the best rise to the top. Although it is a blessing to become a published writer, you can see that it also takes a lot of hard work to get there and that there are practical considerations which can't be ignored. Now that you are fully warned, approach the obstacles head-on. The more you know about the hurdles, the more accurately you can jump them.

The Content

Be wary of writing about personal journeys, vision quests, and stories of survival and triumph. These types of manuscripts often mean a lot to the author but, unfortunately, have little market appeal. Many publishers and agents will not look at such books unless the story is truly extraordinary. It is also unlikely that a mainstream publisher will consider a reinterpretation of a great religious work unless you have relevant scholarly credentials.

People who read books have an agenda: They want to be entertained, uplifted, motivated, or given new information. They choose books that they can relate to. Books have the power to raise consciousness and to reach people on an emotional level, but the material can't be so personal to you that it has no meaning to anyone else.

Spotting Trends

As a spiritual writer, pay attention to the marketplace and educate yourself about the climate of the publishing industry before you shop your book around. Writers sometimes see trends that are in sync with what they want to write. But if you see a lot of books on your topic, you are probably well behind the trend. There may still be a window for a book that presents a fresh perspective, but if you sense that a topic has been exhaustively presented, move on to something else. Aim to spot emerging trends so that the timing of your book will be just right.

You can notice trends by simply observing life. Spiritual writers are blessed with intuition that can help them see beyond what is in front of their face. Look beyond the obvious and try to see how everything relates to everything else. We are all connected. Observation is the key.

There are resources that can help as well. *American Demographics* magazine and books on trend forecasting and marketing such as *The Popcorn Report: Faith Popcorn on the Future of Your Company, Your World, Your Life* and *Clicking: Seventeen Trends That Drive Your Business* (HarperBusiness) by Faith Popcorn are worth studying. Books such as *The Cultural Creatives: How Fifty Million People Are Changing the World* by Paul Ray and Sherry Ruth Anderson (Three Rivers Press, 2001) are invaluable to understand the demographics of the audience interested in spirituality.

You can learn about what is important to people by talking to strangers. You probably already know how to strike up conversations in the checkout line and how to listen to other people's conversations. Just make sure you are discreet! Frequent bookstores and talk to customers and clerks to get a feel for what is selling.

Most, if not all, popular trends started out in an alternative subculture. To put yourself on the cutting edge of trends before they're trends, read print and e-zines (again, see "Spirit-Friendly Resources" for useful sites) and check out alternative magazines at your local independent book or magazine seller. Read popular-culture magazines and watch tele-vision—but use discretion here, because these types of media sometimes aim to create markets rather than cater to them. From television and popular magazines, you can often learn more about what does *not* work. The shows that flop and the products that fail are good indicators of how the public is feeling. And don't ignore yourself. What is important to you? It is likely important to other people as well.

When you have completed an informal look at trends, check to see what books are coming up in the publishing pipeline. Bowker's *Books in Print* has all upcoming titles listed. It's available on-line or in print in the reference section at most libraries. Amazon.com is also a great place to learn about books, including reviews from prominent magazines as well as reviews by readers and detailed descriptions of books' contents.

Request the catalogs of publishers that issue books similar in topic and scope to yours. These catalogs are usually available approximately six months before the books hit the stores and are sometimes available by calling or e-mailing the publisher. As catalogs are expensive to produce, however, not all publishers will mail them to individuals. If this is the case at a house you are interested in, you could ask your local librarian if they are done with their copy. Believe it or not, this can work. Most publishers send their catalogs to libraries hoping to make sales in this market, and librarians seem to have little need of old catalogs. If you are unable to obtain one at all, you can usually get much of the same information from the publisher's Web site.

Go to the sources the publishing industry uses. Prominent review publications such as *Publishers Weekly, Booklist,* and the *New York Times Book Review* are filled with invaluable information about changes in the industry as well as books currently being highlighted by specific publishers. They also include some good general-interest publishing articles, including analyses of popular genres and trends.

Book clubs such as One Spirit and trade magazines such as *New Age Retailer* and *NAPRA ReView,* the publication of the Networking Alternatives for Publishers, Retailers, and Artists can show you clearly what trends exist in your genre. *Writer's Digest* lists upcoming writers' conferences. If you are in the position to do so, you might consider attending one of these in order to make a firm commitment. At many conferences, for the price of admission or a small extra fee, you get face-time with editors and agents who will look at your work and tell you what works for them and what doesn't.

Think of yourself as a detective seaching for clues to what people in the industry already know. By combining keen observation with your link to your spirit and intuition, you should be able to find your niche. You know you need to write—you just need to find where your spirit fits in and how to best give it form in the spiritual marketplace.

A Note about Self-Publishing

In the face of all these challenges, self-publishing may seem to be an easy alternative to playing the "trying to get published game." One advantage is the immediate gratification of going ahead and printing your book without having to wait. Another is having control over every aspect of your work. This freedom, however, is also a costly disadvantage, because writers with no publishing experience have little understanding of how much behind-the-scenes collaboration is necessary to produce the quality books you see in stores. On your own you can't benefit from the greater experience, resources, and contacts of a publisher's established infrastructure. Very few distributors will consider books with the typically amateurish typography, design, and printing of a self-published book. It can cost you thousands of dollars to publish an unpolished piece that you must either distribute by hand mostly to your friends and relatives or leave sitting in boxes in your garage.

The bottom line is this: There is no easy way to get published—just a different distribution of energies. We all know that determination can realize success even under the most trying circumstances. But be sure if you choose this path that you aren't simply trading the work of honing your message and learning to accept criticism from others for learning the publishing industry from the ground up and trying to hand-sell your book on your own.

Developing Credibility

Writers of spiritual nonfiction have another challenge: developing credibility so that someone will want to read what they have to say. No one is going to read a book just because the author claims to have been given a calling to write from the divine source of all creation. When editors see a manuscript that makes unsubstantiated claims from a writer who has no readily apparent spiritual background, they immediately throw it into a box that some people call "woo-woo."

This may happen even if they really like what you have to say. In rare instances they may consider your submission if it is well written, but they will have to overcome the hurdle of convincing the marketing department that you are a writer who people will want to read. Remember, readers have to make an effort to buy a book. Before they will even open it, they need to find something compelling in the book's marketing package to convince them that the author is qualified to write about the message that intrigues them.

So, in a way, before you can expect to be published, you have to prove yourself and pay your dues, just like actors have to work summer stock and perform in small theaters before they can become successful. "Overnight success" only happens in the movies.

Once while working as an agent with an author to develop her book, I came to feel that she was not "ripe" enough in the spiritual understanding of her message and had not yet developed her credibility. We lost touch. Five years later, I ran into her at Book Expo America, the annual trade show for the publishing industry. She had found a major publisher to release her book. It had taken her five years to grow her manuscript and to develop her credibility. We hugged and she said to me with a knowing smile, "It was time." Her energy was relaxed and confident. When I knew her five years earlier, she had been frenetic in her need to have the book published. She felt it had to be published *now*.

She had felt the rumblings in the universe and wanted to fulfill her mission. But it was taken care of when the time was right. Had she not been open to what she, unknowingly, had to learn in order to take her place among published spiritual writers, she might have become frustrated and given up altogether. This is what happens if we do not open ourselves to the challenges we must overcome—we make it much more difficult in the long run. Understand, she was not necessarily having difficulty with her faith, or her spiritual path, which she pursued with love and openness. She was having trouble with the limitations of time, space, and the publishing biz.

How do you establish your credibility as a writer and as a spiritual "expert"? Well, artists create portfolios; you can develop writing credits. Write for any publication that will publish you: magazines, newspapers (daily and weekly), on-line forums, newsletters—but don't expect to make your living this way.

Meet people in your field. Go to workshops. If you are able to connect with people writing the type of books you are interested in writing, you may find some mentors. Better yet, you may find some endorsements. Many of these writers teach at writers' conferences, and many of them hold their own workshops.

Join a speakers' group, such as Toastmasters. After you have developed your speaking skills and are confident of your presentation, speak to any group who will have you. Consider self-publishing your book, and then sell your books after your presentation. These "back of the room" sales figures sometimes impress publishers when you present your manuscript for their consideration. It shows that you know how to generate buzz and are savvy enough to have a saleable message.

If you can, get some media training (that is, training in speaking extemporaneously before a microphone or camera and using bodily and facial gestures to good effect) and develop a speaking "hook," a two- to three-line sentence that encapsulates what your message is about (for more, see part two). Use this hook to promote yourself to radio and television producers, and create a flyer or brochure that encapsulates a tiny portion of your message—the hook that will leave them wanting more and will ensure you a booking on their show.

Develop a press kit that describes your message and your credentials and send it to local television and radio interviewers and news organizations to establish yourself as a speaker on your subject. The media are always looking for "experts," so let them know you're out there and available to comment on news related to your topic. In your press materials, do not emphasize your unpublished book; rather, present a show idea for them and demonstrate that you are an expert in delivering a unique perspective and wealth of information on that particular spiritual topic.

Develop your spiritual credibility by studying with teachers, reading what others have written, and working to connect to your own higher consciousness through prayer and writing. To fully "cook" spiritually, you need to experience life and learn about yourself.

Learn to accept rejection, and *never* denigrate anyone else's success. What goes around comes around. Focus on the positives of what you are doing, not how important you are for doing it. You are not the only one with a mission. Help others, and you help yourself. There is enough to go around.

This sounds like an awful lot of work. I know: I taught spirituality and writing classes for over ten years before I was able to write this book. My spirituality classes helped me hone my message as I taught others, and I gained the value of others' feedback and insights. I have also been teaching at writers' conferences for almost as many years, some on strictly left-brained topics such as book-proposal writing, no spirituality mentioned.

You don't have to wait until you are a household name before submitting a manuscript—although that can't hurt. Just do what you can to enhance your chances. View this groundwork as part of the excitement of the total picture. Every positive effort you make will benefit you down the road, no matter when you are published.

Staying Humble

Worthiness is often a big issue for spiritual writers: either we are not worthy of our message, like the rabbi, or we are *too* worthy, *too* special. Beware of trying to gain credibility by drawing attention to yourself. This "look at me" attitude can come across as arrogance. Keep your focus and your faith. You do not have to sell God and you do not have to sell yourself. While you do have to promote yourself in order to be heard, don't forget that you are a conduit for spirit. Spirit will find its place and its audience if given enough exposure.

As the conduit, you are not irrelevant to the process, but if you are too concerned with making sure that audiences know how special and spiritually evolved you are, you will either alienate them or mislead them to think that you are more important than your words. Help people see their own spiritual potential through you. If you are looking to be worshipped, then you may have difficulty progressing on your path. You may be terrific and successful, but you will not be representing a spiritual message or helping others build a spiritual connection.

We all typically go through variations of the "look at me" stage. God knows I have, and sometimes still do, because it's human nature to seek validation. But if we are too needy in this way—and who isn't to some extent?—we might end up trying too hard and instead work against ourselves.

Many of the lessons spiritual writers learn relate to this issue of accepting themselves without needing everyone's approval. If we seek only external validation, we are going to write for this purpose, and this self-consciousness will show in our writing. If we work toward self-acceptance, we are then building a better connection with ourselves and our God, which will in turn allow us to better accomplish our mission. When we are able to accept and love ourselves, we can write from a place that has room for spirit.

I struggled for years with a desire to share what I had learned about spirituality with others and to write about it. When I was a very new writer and an even newer student of spirituality, religion, and metaphysics, I was jealous of anyone who had published a book on the subject. In my deluded grandeur, I believed I could do as well as they and deserved the attention they were receiving. The flip side of this inflated sense of myself was a total lack of confidence. While I was able to write articles and books on topics that did not reflect my deepest spiritual beliefs, I could not find the right language to reflect those beliefs that were most important to me. When we battle ourselves, we can't write and we can't grow.

Spiritual writers can become caught up in the progress on our path as if it were some kind of competition. But we aren't going to "win" by owning the most holy relics, preaching the loudest, or wearing the most crystals. We are perpetual students; even the most enlightened person can experience spiritual arrogance in which the need to be noticed outweighs the importance of the message he is trying to convey. If we get stuck on the need for the world to conform to our particular understanding of the meaning of life, we can become blocked. We might suffer over every word because we want to show the editor just how much we know about the subject and how important it is that she listen to us.

One time during a particularly grueling writing session when I had twisted my hair into a spring, my husband approached me and whispered in my ear, "Stop worrying so much. You are not writing the Bible." I felt like a woman in labor trying to resist the urge to fling a heavy object at his head. But he was right.

Finding Your Voice

We are all essentially on our own when it comes to our spiritual path. No two people occupy the same path at the same time. We may simply walk side by side and offer help to each other. But we are separate in physical form from one another for a reason: We each have a unique voice and spark to add to the light of everyone else. The trick is to find it.

Writers who avoid a flashy, attention-getting style of writing can more easily relax and write with a natural voice. Self-conscious writing is as obvious to an audience as when an actor loses his character on the stage. While watching television talk shows, such as Rosie O'Donnell or Oprah Winfrey, we are entertained because even though the host is the focal point of the show, she welcomes us as if we were part of an intimate gathering. We feel a sense of inclusion rather than the self-consciousness of an intruder.

When you write a spiritual book, remember that spiritual seekers are going to buy and read it because they either need or want something. They want to be educated, they want to solve a problem or mystery, or they want to be inspired. When people buy spiritual books, they want to share an experience with the writer not unlike a student-teacher relationship. If the writer overwrites every sentence to make himself seem more knowledgeable and important than he really is, the reader will feel this and be uncomfortable.

Readers want to feel cared about and important. They aren't interested in reading about how important someone else is. They expect that a book written by a spiritual guru will be about how the reader can have a better life, not about how enlightened the guru is. Spiritual teachers whose philosophies have evolved through many turns on their own paths do not have to brag about their specialness. They know where inspiration and wisdom come from. They know the secret that we all have the same potential and right to be awake and aware of the truth.

The further along on the path, the more information they may have to share. This has nothing to do with craft and success but has everything to do with conveying a pure spiritual message. The more we get out of our own way and work through our human issues on the path to self-awareness, the better messengers we make. The message is more pure if it is not filtered through our need for attention. Our message can become distorted when self-awareness becomes less important than self-promotion.

Knowing When It's Good Enough

We all know that life isn't always easy, and it is definitely not a straight line. I often define spiritual awakening as the act of being hit by a two-by-four on the head, and I define the writer's journey as the process of wanting to tell everyone how it feels.

We do not have to be "healed" or to have achieved total self-awareness to write good spiritual books. In fact, our process toward awareness is often the most important thing we can share. This is how we help each other along the way. There comes a time when we have to decide that our writing is good enough. If we wait for our own perfection, we will not write.

Jennifer, a friend of mine, is a talented writer, but she doesn't believe it. In fact, she does not believe she is pretty, intelligent, or at times even likable. She worries that she is not sufficiently spiritual—she doesn't meditate enough, doesn't go to church often enough, doesn't do enough good deeds, and on and on. She is a lovable and wonderful friend, so I haven't strangled her yet for her negative attitude, but I regret that she holds herself back from her other dreams and creative endeavors because of it. And I know that her self-consciousness is typical and that many of us have to overcome this obstacle, because it's simply a lesson of life—particularly with any creative undertaking.

In summary, do not rely on how loud you can yell about yourself. And do not worry that you are not worthy of sharing your message—you are! You just need to learn the protocols of the publishing industry and work hard to take your place among the messengers. You can do it. There can never be too many spiritual writers. Your triumph benefits us all.

EASTER
BASKETS —
TREAT SMILES

I ALWAYS WANTED MORE TO EAT —
NOT ~~~~ MORE ~~~ JUST THE TREATS:

I NEVER MEANT THAT I'D COMMIT —
A LIFETIME DIETS JUST OF IT.

3

SEVEN LESSONS OF THE SPIRIT

Using the seemingly random events of our lives as object lessons, we can learn both how to be the best human we can be and how to awaken our spirituality. Through my study of religion, in observing fellow writers, and through life itself, I have noted that each of us typically experiences seven universal life lessons. Some of these lessons will be more or less relevant at different times, but all are ultimately integrated into our lives. The seven lessons are *courage, tolerance, self-protection, self-love, ego, love of humanity,* and *God-love.* Each helps us make sense of how we are to go about our unique tasks; each gives us a hint of how we can create balance in our lives as a practicing human and a practicing writer.

These lessons remind us that we do not act in a void. Everything we do has an impact on everyone else. The thoughts and words that we bring into the world possess an energy that exists far beyond us. We need to be aware of this responsibility and also confident enough to allow ourselves to accept the gift of writing. As we write, we are nourished by the spirit of God and the love that is directed at the world. In turn, we can nourish others, who return the blessing again to us. It is an endless circle.

Descriptions of the following lessons are intentionally minimal so that you will turn to your intuition to define their relevance in your own journey. Later in the chapter, I use them as jumping-off points for journal exercises.

Courage

The call to write is not only a privilege but also a guarantee that you will likely never be able to fully participate in a so-called "normal" life. Writers view life through a different lens than others, and a spiritual writer views it through the added dimension of spirit. Spiritual awareness is a good thing, but it can also be lonely when you perceive that you are different from others.

So one of our challenges as spiritual writers is to resist the natural desire to fit in. We often try to do everything in our power to deny the intuitive wisdom knocking on our soul. Because we can be in perpetual conflict with ourselves and the institutions and people in our lives, spiritual writers are given lessons in courage all the time. While our spirit asks us to serve the greater good through our writing, the loneliness and exposure this brings can be terrifying.

One of the most powerful lessons of courage comes when we realize that what we know and what we have been taught are not reconcilable. Do you remember when you first began to question what you then took for spiritual truth? These questions do not mean that our teachers were wrong but rather that we are driven toward a more personal spiritual path. We have to experience faith for ourselves to understand it within our souls; we can't simply adopt another's version of it. If we as spiritual writers are to be teachers, we must first accept, with courage, our role as students. This often brings us into conflict with loved ones and friends as we take charge of our own direction. Human beings are like pack animals. We don't like to do things alone, and the pack has a way of discouraging those who try to go their own way. But as the spiritual writer learns very early, to experience spirit in a personal way, you need to have the courage to explore. Each path has room for one traveler. We can be parallel to each other but cannot take up the same space at the same time.

We are given lessons in courage at every turn, because to write from spirit we need to seek truth, to support it, and to commit to it by putting it in a concrete form: our writing. Once we write something down, it no longer belongs to us. We send it into the world as we do our children. We cannot control how it is received, and we have to accept any consequences associated with it.

We can write simply to please others, but that doesn't take courage. The challenge lies in taking the circumstances—lessons—you are given that will push your spirit to show its true self, your highest self. And as your soul progresses, your awareness grows.

Tolerance

When we find our personal truth and have the courage to write about it, we can become overly exuberant, like a happily married person who tries to fix up all of her friends just so they can be "happy" too. We become spiritual matchmakers. So the lesson of tolerance is particularly important for spiritual writers, as it teaches us to allow people to pursue their own truth at their own pace.

Tolerance is not antithetical to our role as spiritual messenger. As messengers, it is important to avoid the pitfall of trying to force people to believe as we believe. This doesn't work anyway. There is no way to force a person to change his inner truth—and why would you want to? Many different paths lead to the same place. If you pressure people into seeing things your way, this is not being a spiritual messenger. It is bullying.

To deliver a message well and with tolerance is to make it available to those who want it, can understand it, or are ready to become illuminated by it.

Another important aspect of tolerance is that it teaches us that we will never know everything. We are always on a path. If we become too smug, we will be reminded that we have feet of clay like everyone else. We need to remember that we all progress at different rates and all have things we need to learn. Tolerance lessons teach us to allow people their own struggle. We all want to help each other, but sometimes too much help will eliminate a person's right to learn a lesson honestly. No one can experience the triumph of self-respect if they do not achieve it on their own.

So, spiritual writers need to maintain boundaries that give people room to grow. If you have children, then you already know, since child-rearing is full of lessons of this kind. For example, one of the most difficult tasks is to allow our children to experience pain. We want them to grow as whole human beings, yet we want to share our years of experience with them so that they do not make the same mistakes— and we can suffocate them with our good intentions. As writers, we have a similar role—of guiding while respecting others' boundaries. We serve the greater good if we present our work humbly and with gratitude, allowing our readers to accept what they need and disregard what does not resonate. We do not own our words; they come through us as gifts from spirit.

Self-Protection

To experience spirit is to experience something that makes perfect sense. It is love, it is acceptance, it is simplicity. We feel connected and we feel safe. Aside from the tolerance pitfalls of wanting everyone to share in our bliss, we tend to let down our guard. We forget to watch our backs.

Lessons of self-protection remind us that we are spiritual beings in a relatively nonspiritual world. Not everyone chooses to progress on a spiritual path. While we do not want to deny them the right to choose, we learn through our self-protection lessons that we have to be vigilant in guarding our energy from others' negativity.

When we awaken to faith, we are filled with love. We observe others who may not be reflecting the potential of their own higher selves.

We dismiss this reality and project a potential onto them. We can become too trusting and sometimes too helpful. We may allow our valuable spiritual energy to be consumed by people who are essentially energy vampires. It is important to learn to conserve our energy and use it only where it will do the most good. In other words, do not chase after those who do not really want what we have to give.

Some self-protection lessons come in the form of learning who to trust or who not to trust. In our eagerness to share our message, we can lose all sense of perspective around certain people and allow them to steer us off our path. Sometimes these people are even those who are closest to us. These lessons can be difficult, as they usually lead to disillusionment or loss. It is up to us to learn how to maintain our balance in light of those people who bring out our vulnerabilities. We can learn to create a shield of sorts around ourselves.

We also are given lessons that teach us about our lack of faith in ourselves. Just because we open ourselves to spirit does not make us invulnerable to our own internal negativity. We may be filled with doubts, fears, and envy of other writers' accomplishments. If we are not careful, our writer's journey can be contaminated by the negativity within us. That is why self-protection lessons are important to spiritual writers, because anything that throws us off our path prevents the purity of our message from reaching its intended audience. And one of our jobs is to shield our vulnerable points so that we do not become vessels for imbalance.

Self-Love

The lessons of self-love have to do with being worthy of love not only from other people but also from our God. This is a lesson spiritual writers need to learn if we are to support our own inner voice. If we require approval from everyone, we are going to write to please others rather than to reflect the spirit inside of us. We can't be a messenger if we do not have faith enough in ourselves to carry out the job. As I discussed earlier, besides causing us to write inauthentically, a constant need for outside validation can also lead to massive writer's block when we realize that we can never be perfect and can never be all things to all people.

We all have differing degrees of self-love, and we are given lessons every day to help us to see how wonderful we are. We all have unique qualities and limitations; they are essential elements in the lessons of our lives. We ourselves are the purveyors of our most challenging self-love lessons. As we have seen, when we write, we want to know that our work is good. We want to be noticed, and we want accolades. Self-love lessons teach us that it isn't necessary to be constantly validated, that our work will never be right for everyone. We may be on a spiritual mission, but we are not being asked to change the world all at once. The lesson of self-love gives us the ability to accept our role in a much larger picture as being all we need to accomplish. We don't even need to be published to have gained love and acceptance from the universe. We will never let the universe down if we do not find a publisher for our book. These lessons are to teach us that our path is for us.

We follow our desire to write books because books are the vehicle through which we give of our spirit to others. This exchange of spirit elevates all souls. Even if we never write an opus or never do anything that we feel other people will notice, the lessons of self-love teach us that our living spirit is enough.

Ego

Ego lessons can be some of the most difficult to learn. As I discussed earlier, staying humble can be particularly difficult for spiritual writers, who sometimes have to struggle to separate themselves from their message. As an agent, I have seen spiritual ego deadlock some potentially important careers. People turn down offers or have unrealistic expectations of their role in their own success because they believe the world is waiting for them. It is so important that spiritual writers do not succumb to the pull of ego.

When we feel the link to spirit, it is natural and easy to become full of ourselves. We believe we are more special and more connected to spirit than other, less evolved humans. Fortunately, ego lessons tend to burst that bubble even before it reaches maximum inflation. The reason is obvious: If you put yourself above others, you essentially put yourself above God. You become the message rather than the messenger.

Rampant spiritual ego causes us to face many risks:

- We can block the message of spirit. Having spiritual ego is a hollow worship of self, which eliminates the possibility of any real love or connection to our spirit.
- We can lead people off their paths. Our role as spiritual writer is to guide people to their *own* spiritual awakening, not to *our* own version of it. We are mentors and want our students to eventually outgrow all that we could ever teach them and ultimately to trust their own inner voice.
- We can become the focal point for the seeker. We make the mistake of thinking that having people become dependent on us is the fulfillment of our role as spiritual teacher.
- We can be easily diverted away from our own path. Spiritual ego cannot coexist with faith. We need to keep the proper balance between service and wanting to be served.

The lessons of ego are presented to every spiritual traveler so that we can learn how important it is to be strong in faith. We are here to help ourselves and each other progress in the growth of our souls and in our awareness of spirit, and we can't assist others on their path if we believe the path leads to us.

Love of Humanity

Spiritual writers often see the potential in all human beings to connect to spirit; we see that we all have a link to the main generator. We draw from the same base of intelligence; we have the same choices, needs, and feelings; and we learn the same lessons.

That said, it still isn't easy to look at the world without judgment. While we can't write to please everyone, we must take care not to write in a way that excludes those whose spiritual path differs from ours, presuming that they are incapable of spiritual growth.

If you write for a particular market, such as Christian or New Age, it is possible to identify yourself with that genre without denigrating other paths. Don't waste energy proving people wrong; give energy to what you believe is right.

Writers never really know who will read our books or whose lives will be influenced by what we write. When we learn the lesson of love of humanity, we become willing to let go of our words so that they will reach whoever needs them. Even though we do not have physical control over our books, we do have spiritual control over how willing we are to give them a life separate from us.

I can be intellectually judgmental. I have had to learn over and over not to do things for people that they can do for themselves. I don't do this out of kindness, necessarily, but because I don't always see their potential. Love of humanity teaches us to stay in our own lives while honoring the lives and abilities of others.

God-Love

When you learn the first six lessons, you remove some of the doubts about your own higher truth. God-love is achieved, for a spiritual writer, when you surrender to your divine inner voice and allow it to work through you.

God-love is the most personal of the seven lessons, providing you with a knowledge of spirit that extends beyond belief. Many of you who are called to write about your spiritual journey know that there came a point at which no one could persuade you away from your faith. The lessons of God-love feed this internal link between mind and spirit.

You will continually encounter spiritual teachers and helpers along the way until you return to spirit yourself. However, you will find that you become more confident in pursuing your own path when you rely only on your own knowledge of truth and God. The lessons of God-love push us out of the proverbial nest, helping us find our true spiritual self. When this happens, we know that we can be true messengers, influenced by what is inside us. We have our own voice to add to the spiritual chorus.

Much of the deepest loneliness we experience stems from our sense of disconnection from God and from other human beings. When we are given lessons of God-love, we are able to feel undeniably that we are never really alone. We are always part of something that guides us through our own lives as we seek to help fellow travelers in their lives as well.

Lessons of God-love help us to overcome fear by teaching us, when we are most afraid, to turn toward spirit. Understanding that our lives are not completely random gives us the comfort we need to fulfill our destiny. There will always be unpredictable events in life, but when we know that we are part of something greater than ourselves and that we share this with all other souls, we can transcend fear and replace it with action. We can participate fully in our lives through spirit.

The Seven-Lessons Journal

A seven-lessons journal is a tool to help you actively grow your soul while gaining awareness of your true self. It helps you become an authentic writer in tune with your divine inner voice. When you look at your life and your writer's journey through the lens of these seven lessons, you can see how you may have repeated some experiences over and over. These lessons lead to awakening. As you proceed with your journaling, you may get to the point where you can feel a lesson take shape. You may not know what to do about it because you aren't sure what you are to learn, but when you experience a lesson, you will be aware that you have changed.

Use these lessons as catalysts to begin a dialogue with your self. Use them to forge a connection to spirit, your inner teacher. Your journal can be a form of meditation, a blessing—whether or not you publish—because it links you with your inner voice and the divine spark. Consider it spiritual therapy. You may be surprised at the words that come forth as you start addressing the journal questions at the end of this chapter.

It is not always easy to learn about yourself. It can be as difficult as trying to edit your own manuscript. Spiritual journaling requires objectivity to avoid dismissing what might need to be changed. On the other hand, it is equally difficult to look at oneself kindly if we are measuring ourselves against perceived spiritual ideals.

Your work as a spiritual writer is meant for popular consumption. But for many spiritual writers, our first books are typically about our inner journey. In all candor, these are the books that mean the most to us but that are the least likely to be published unless we have a major following or are an extraordinary writer. I have a first book sealed in shrink-wrap which is so personal that I will likely never show it to anyone—not even my mother!

Not all first manuscripts should be shrink-wrapped. If you think yours should be shared with the world, the rest of this book will show you how to submit it for publication. However, if you write in your journal using the seven lessons as guidelines while you experience a process of spiritual self-discovery, you may get some things out of your system so you can work on a first book that may be more commercially viable.

These lessons will also help keep you grounded in how to live spiritually in this world. We are not here to learn how to be spirit. We already are. Your journal writing will help you learn how to integrate your spirit with your daily life so you can contribute not only to the growth of your soul but to the process of soul evolution for everyone.

Create a sacred space for yourself to write in your journal. If you are most comfortable with a computer, there is no reason this cannot represent your sacred space. If you are a pen-and-paper sort of person, set aside several notebooks for journaling. I like composition books, but there are many other wonderful ways to create a special journal to hold your thoughts and feelings. The main thing is to set the time aside to truly dialogue, to open up a portal between you and spirit.

When you first begin your journal, make a list of the seven lessons on the first page, using your intuition to determine which lessons have had the greatest influence on your life. If you believe you have passed through or beyond a particular lesson, indicate this by writing *yes* next to it. Write *no* if you believe you have yet to learn or complete a particular lesson. Do not use your left brain; write your first response, as intellectualizing can prevent us from being honest with ourselves. You might be surprised with your intuitive answers, which will give you some material to discuss in your journal.

Sometimes opening an inspirational book will yield answers that can help you decide if you have learned a lesson from a subconscious level. Don't be nervous if you feel that you have not yet learned anything. The lessons are simply a guide for your path. There is no time limit, and you can't be expelled from the school of spirit. You may have to repeat a grade—as I have done many times—but you will always be measured against your awareness of your self. You are not in competition. You are looking for illumination, balance, and spiritual connection.

And you will find answers. You can be totally honest in your journals because there is no judgment in the world of spirit, only unconditional love and guidance. Spirit knows what is in your heart, even with the limitations of language. What you write is for you. You are safe. You are loved. You are free to be your true self.

Allow yourself plenty of time. Your journals are not a luxury. Your spiritual path and your writer's journey are the basis for your existence. While you attend to the responsibilities of your daily life, you must not forget to nourish your spirit. Don't feel guilty about your journaling because you think you should be writing your book or proposal or doing something else useful. As you may have already discovered, with the awareness that journal-writing brings and the way it exercises your voice, your writing will be easier and better with the journal than without.

And when you choose to take care of your daily responsibilities, don't feel guilty that you are not writing in your journal. You have a lifetime to explore and to grow in spirit and in your writing. This is a journal you can keep until your final moments on earth, and you will always learn something new. I would never want to give a fellow writer a reason to be more neurotic and anxious than we already tend to be! It takes a certain amount of anxiety and adrenaline to write in the first place, so don't waste it worrying about your journal.

It can be really productive to begin journal-writing sessions with a prayer, a special thought, or some kind of affirmation to center yourself. Read scripture, do some deep breathing, stretch, pet your cat—anything that makes you feel calm and focused.

But there can also be benefits to writing when you are the least centered. Sometimes it is great to write while you are agitated. Anger at life and at God or others is certainly part of the rhythm of life and also has a place in your journal. Throw some pots if you want to. Scream! The spiritual path is not all rainbows, ethereal music, or even fellowship.

Follow along with your lessons as if they are a translation of the language of your life. Your willingness to accept your challenges and to learn from them will directly influence your path. This is not all hindsight. Why repeat lessons if you can learn them? Awareness allows you to make different decisions the next time.

Before you begin this part of your writer's journey, I would like to leave you with this prayer:

> *May the beloved creator of your understanding*
> *be with you on your spiritual and writer's journey.*
> *And may these lessons and exercises give you*
> *the insights and confidence you need to sustain you on your path.*

Exercises

Each time you write in your journal, choose one of the seven lessons, and then ask yourself a question, such as those below. Of course, you don't have to start off with a question. Sometimes contemplation or anger can reveal things that you had not considered. As with everything spiritual, get out of the way. Let your spirit be free. Find your true voice and connection with the divine.

1. Have there been examples of this lesson in my life?
2. Have I learned this lesson?
3. Do I have more to learn?
4. What were the circumstances around this lesson?
5. Have I experienced this lesson before?
6. Why do I keep repeating this lesson?
7. What does this lesson mean to me?
8. How do the qualities implied by this lesson influence my writer's journey?

9. What do I see as my vulnerabilities?

10. What can I learn from this lesson?

11. How can this lesson change how I live my life?

12. When did I first believe in my own ideas over others?

13. Have I had to defend my beliefs?

14. What is my personal mission and what obstacles do I face in carrying it out?

15. Have I ever felt resistance from a person but persisted only to get nowhere?

16. How has God been present in my life today?

17. Can I see a pattern in my circumstances?

18. Am I being aware of others around me and setting firm boundaries?

19. Am I reinforcing my worthiness to be loved? Am I taking care of myself in a loving way?

20. Am I keeping my ego in balance? Am I reminding myself that I am a messenger and not the message?

21. Do I see the light of God in other people? Do I have empathy?

22. Do I have faith that my life is not random but rather part of a connected web of God's light?

Part Two
FROM INSPIRATION TO MANUSCRIPT

Having the inspiration to write and knowing what you want to write about does not automatically mean you have even the slightest idea about the mechanics of writing a publishable book. No one is born with this knowledge, so don't be discouraged if you haven't been able to pull out your trusty computer, the one you purchased just for this occasion, to begin your opus without hesitation.

The intent of the next four chapters is to demystify the process of writing a complete manuscript by breaking it into discrete steps. As discussed in the previous chapters, it can be challenging for spiritual writers to make the transition from the excitement of inspiration to the sometimes tedious minutiae of creating a marketable, publishable product. Can your spirituality be squeezed into these publishing parameters? Of course it can!

Chapter 4, "Transforming Inspiration into an Angle," gives you pointers on what publishing professionals look for in a proposal and manuscript and the special challenges of distilling a spiritual message into a few lines of text. Those few lines, often called your angle or hook, are perhaps the most important element of the whole package that you'll submit to an agent or publisher. It condenses your message so that the many people who will potentially read it will know instantly what it is you're writing about and whether you have a marketable idea.

Chapter 5, "Finding Your Genre," will help you further tether your message to the realities of publishing by asking you to define yourself and your idea: What genre does your manuscript fall into and where would it be shelved in a bookstore?

Many spiritual writers feel that their message is pure, and they often write with abandon and passion. Chapter 6, "Can Spirit Be Contained in an Outline?" will help you see how to keep the passion while still creating an organized, logically flowing manuscript.

Lastly, in chapter 7, "Writing and Editing," we'll discuss how to make your now-finished draft the best it can be before you send it out into the publishing world.

4

TRANSFORMING INSPIRATION INTO AN ANGLE

In your journal, you can allow your thoughts to roam free. You can ramble to your heart's content. However, when you sit down to write a book for someone else to read, you need to harness all that free-floating inspiration and funnel it into a concise message that makes sense to other people. That message, which is the essence of all that you wish to convey, is your hook.

A hook is as it sounds: something the reader can hang on to—one or two sentences at the most. This hook is your *thesis*, which Webster's defines as "a position or proposition that a person advances and offers to maintain by argument." This seems simple, but it may actually be one of the most complicated aspects of the book-writing process. The goal is to encapsulate your entire book into one or two sentences to convey your idea with pinpoint accuracy. If you are unable to do this, your idea needs further refinement and focus. Some people start with a hook and then write, but usually your hook will evolve as your message takes shape.

A clear hook puts you in control of how, to some extent, a reader will receive and interpret your message. Of course, reading is as much an active process as writing, and every reader brings a different set of preconceptions to a manuscript, but a clearly elucidated thesis orients the reader to what you are about to say instead of to perhaps what he thinks you are saying.

Imagine meeting your dream editor in an elevator. You have thirty seconds, between floors three and twenty-three, to pitch your book and convince her that you have a marketable idea. That's about as much time as you'll get when your submission lands on someone's desk. So make every word count!

Agents and acquisitions editors typically only scan submissions. Most agents, editors, and even interns will not dig through poorly organized or thought-out manuscripts. They aren't going to work that hard when they have so many proposals to consider, and they will be more attracted to those that make their jobs easier. Some manuscript reviewers become so overwhelmed with the backlog of unread submissions that they actually are relieved when they can find a reason to reject a manuscript and move on to the next one in their pile. Don't let a lame or fuzzy hook be the reason your manuscript gets tossed into the "No" box from which, eventually, an intern will retrieve it to send you a nice rejection letter. It is as simple as that. Unless you are a major celebrity whose name alone is enough to sell a book, an agent or editor is not going to spend time trying to figure out what it is you are trying to say.

Good Bones Make for a Good Hook

The ancient editorial axiom states, "You can't get a good hook from a rotten idea." So be brutally honest with yourself; look your muse in the face and ask, "Is this book idea of mine something that anyone else would want to read?" Then take your muse to the library or on-line to see if there are other books on your topic; if there are, great! This means competition, yes, but it also means that publishers have seen a demand for the topic.

When you have determined that there appears to be a market, then work on developing your hook. Here's the hook for this book:

The special challenge for spiritual writers is to accommodate the commercial needs of publishers without losing sight of their mission. While focusing on such practical aspects of getting published as query letters, proposals, editing, and finding spirit-friendly agents and publishers, the book also guides the reader through seven obstacles spiritual writers commonly encounter.

This is a strong hook for two reasons: first, because it encapsulates what the entire book is about—every chapter, every paragraph, and even every sentence relates back to this thesis—and second, from a marketing standpoint, because while there are many "how to get published" books out there, not one is directed specifically to spiritual writers and their unique needs.

Fifty-four words. An entire book boiled down to almost nothing but vapor. I am not a woman of few words, and it was not easy to develop such a focused thesis statement. But as you see, it can be done! If your idea has not evolved enough to boil it down to its essence, try outlining its major topic areas or even writing free-form. Inspiration is not static. If you play with your idea through journal-writing or writing a rough draft or outline of your manuscript, you may find that the real hook pops out to greet you. As in any kind of writing, you may think you are writing one book when actually there is another book inside you waiting to be birthed.

You will know you have found your hook when you can visualize or otherwise sense your manuscript in its entirety. You may see chapter titles and subsections within them; you may see how you will build your manuscript, from beginning to end. Even though you don't know the specific words that will fill the pages, your search for a hook has brought you to the outline of your manuscript.

If you write fiction, the hook is just as important, but it is presented differently, typically as the journey of your protagonist. Someone looking at a synopsis of your book needs to understand enough by your concise plot summary and description of the significant conflicts to be resolved to know immediately if they want to read farther.

Here are some examples of hooks from successful spiritual titles:

- *Journey of Souls: Case Studies of Life Between Lives* by Michael Duff Newton. A controversial exploration of what happens after we die based on actual cases where Newton regresses his patients to a point between lives—after death but before birth.
- *The Mystical Mind: Probing the Biology of Religious Experience* by Eugene G. D'Aquili and Andrew B. Newberg. Two leading medical researchers explore how the physiology of the brain is involved in the religious and mystical experience.
- *The World Is as You Dream It: Shamanic Teachings from the Amazon and Andes* by John Perkins. An acclaimed environmentalist, teacher, and activist studied with South American shamanic teachers who introduced him to their rituals and religious beliefs about healing, dreaming, psychotropic drugs, and magic.
- *In the Meantime: Finding Yourself and the Love You Want* by Iyanla Vanzant. How the "meantime" of daily struggle is the work we are called to do on ourselves so we can make the most of our lives.

A Good Hook Lives On and On

The life of a good synopsis doesn't end with your writing the manuscript and proposal. Assuming your proposal merits a closer look, editors will read your manuscript to see if it delivers what the hook promises. Or if you're lucky enough to have your proposal accepted before you've written the entire manuscript, a strong hook ensures a mutual vision between the editor and writer so the finished product reflects everyone's overall intent. It keeps things on track.

Throughout the sales process, a strong hook allows publishers and their distributors to sell the book with clarity and enthusiasm. When a new book is pitched to a publisher's sales staff, its distributor, or to retail booksellers, there is no time for long-winded explanations. Everyone is busy. Each book merits just a few minutes to establish its worthiness, or rather, its sales potential. A great hook gives everyone in the process a tool to describe the book completely and succinctly to their customers.

5

FINDING YOUR GENRE

Your writer's voice emanates from your inner muse, reflecting your unique style, perspective, and soul. It cannot be duplicated by anyone. As individual as it is, though, it must conform to what readers expect from the genre in which you are writing. For example, a business-advice book on how women can break through the glass ceiling would call for a friendly but authoritative and knowledgeable voice; details and specific advice and directives would take precedence over the author's personal revelations or musings. The audience would want to feel they were in the hands of an expert who had specific recommendations to help them.

A spiritual book, on the other hand, can generally assume a more intimate tone, almost as one friend giving loving advice to another. The reader is seeking a relationship, both with you, as the author, and with the material. She wants to know in what way it is relevant to her life. Because the topic is not about a specific subject but the core of life and experience itself, a spiritual book requires a greater connection between the author and reader.

So no matter what the topic you write about, strive to reveal your authentic voice—the expression of the contents of your soul. When your writing feels natural and honest to you, you are writing with your true voice; you are so connected to your mind that your words convey the full and clear reflection of your message.

No one can write anything, not even the copy for a box of cereal, if they are self-conscious about every word. Let your voice emerge without editing. That part will come later. If you engage your intellect too early in the process, it will be like trying to water your garden while someone is kinking up the hose.

Self-Revelation

In any kind of writing, the author's task is to help the reader enjoy the content without too much interference, so the reader can escape into it. This is a fine line. In spiritual books, you want to reveal enough of yourself to establish the vital connection between you and the reader—but not too much. After all, the reader is looking in your book not for insights into *your* life but for a better understanding of his own.

While a certain amount of self-revelation and a warm, inviting tone can help establish your credentials and voice, unless the work is a memoir or autobiography—which must be absolutely exceptional to work for the general public—self-disclosure must be kept to a minimum. Avoid filling your work with such personal details that it causes the reader to feel like she has accidentally walked into your personal therapy session. A reader should feel like she is part of things, not like an outsider.

Similarly, the reader is looking to learn from your book, but she doesn't want to feel like a spiritual dunce. If you write a book that makes your life appear special and amazing, it creates the impression that no one else is living a life half as extraordinary. Your life may indeed be compelling or it would not make for even the most skeletal of books, but every life is extraordinary—it is all in the telling. So strive to include your reader as a welcome and respected participant.

When you write for your own personal empowerment—in your journal or for your own memoirs—let your voice be big, strong, free, powerful, and personal. If you want to write for publication, however, be sure to include the reader at your party and make your voice less personal and more inclusive of others' experiences. Later, when you become a household name, people *might* want to know every little thing about you. Until then, do not make your book so personal that no one will want to read it except your mother.

Letting Your Voice Emerge

When you sit down to write, you may know so much about where you are heading that you could write your book practically overnight. You take your outline and place it on a bulletin board where you can see it. You stretch out your fingers, crack your neck, and begin to write. What comes out is something you do not recognize. You can hear it in your mind. It sounds like someone is talking while you are writing, but it isn't you.

Oh, but if it were any good! I can't speak for anyone else, but when I write it takes a while to find a voice that sounds like me. I actually hear a voice in my head when I get started. Sometimes the voice starts as a stuffy lawyer or as a professor writing on a subject I don't know how to teach. The more I relax and get warmed up, the more natural it sounds. Other times, if I am writing spiritual material, I hear a voice that is so ethereal that I can't understand a word she is saying. It comes out fast, but I need a spiritual translator to figure it out.

And sometimes I practically glue myself to a chair and still cannot find my natural voice. I wind up rewriting the same thing over and over, hitting the delete key with mounting frustration. These rejects are not edited versions of something good; they are the product of total mental constipation.

As I mentioned earlier, I believe the reason writers get stuck is that we lack confidence. We worry inordinately about pleasing some fictitious reader who wants to hate our work. It may sound a little paranoid, but few of us ever think that someone reading our work actually wants to find what is good in it. Not true! The readers you're interested in having read your book *want* to like what you write. They are looking for insights. Publishers and agents do too, because then they can generate sales.

So you may as well relax. If you are pursuing a spiritual path and are inspired to write, your writing stems from a place of truth. To find your voice, put yourself in the proper frame of mind by writing down or repeating to yourself these affirmations:

- I have something unique and special to say.
- My writing is inspired.
- Readers will love my true voice.
- Writing brings me inner peace.

Add to this list anything which makes you realize that you have nothing to be afraid of. Your voice needs to be heard!

So, to find your voice, let go of control of the process. Don't edit as you go along. Concentrate on revealing your message, not your life history. After you allow your inner voice to emerge with all its exuberance and imperfections, you can go back later and correct any flaws. Computer technology, with its wonderful delete key and cut-and-paste function, is a blessing for the spiritual writer who needs to first unleash and then later temper the spirit.

If you find that no matter what you do, everything comes out certifiably terrible, take a break and objectively ask yourself if you are caught up in the result rather than the process. There is always a lesson to be learned by strong feelings. I firmly believe that if we are operating on a voice-disconnect, anything we write will need to be rewritten anyway. If this happens, set your writing aside and work on something else for a while.

What Kind of Spiritual Writer Are You?

A crucial step in finding your voice is knowing what kind of spiritual writer you are, that is, what genre your writing falls into. For example, booksellers categorize spirituality, religion, New Age, occult practices, psychic phenomena, UFOs, and ghosts separately. All are spiritual—some to a greater extent than others—but each appeals to vastly different audiences. Christian books are a separate and substantial market; the term is used in publishing to define books that deal with life issues and spiritual topics from a strongly Christian, often biblically based perspective. In publishing, books that are categorized as Christian differ from those shelved under "religion," which refers primarily to scholarly and historically researched books. Inspiration is yet another category; it often includes gift books that are packaged as much for visual appeal as for content.

Naturally, many of these categories overlap, because books often fit more than one description and also because some categories, such as New Age, are becoming less distinct as the topics become more mainstream. We're going to look at the six most common nonfiction spiritual categories: spirituality, religion, New Age, Christian, inspirational, and occult; an article about visionary fiction follows. If your book doesn't quite fit into any of these genres yet still seems as though it should be under the general spiritual umbrella, refer to "Spirit-Friendly Resources" for some research ideas.

Spirituality

Publishers define general spirituality books as those about self-transformation and a greater understanding of the divine or life force. This category also encompasses books that stress the connection humans have to all aspects of life as well as the power of changing one's consciousness.

Religion

This refers primarily to research-based books about the major world religions. Here, an author's credentials are important, such as formal religious or philosophical education or training. You will not find non-credentialed writers in this genre.

New Age

New Age developed as a catchall category for topics that did not fit anywhere else, some of which, like yoga or meditation, have become so mainstream in the past twenty years that they are hardly new at all. New Age books cover transformation, meditation, channeling, pyramids, ancient mysticism, shamanism, Native American spirituality, crystals, alternative health (which sometimes occupies its own category), energy work, and spiritualism.

In the 1980s, New Age authors examined the existence of realities beyond our physical world and religious institutions, such as angels, distance healing, and auras. Today, there has been a shift from books marveling at the existence of these phenomena to books that show their application in our lives, thus creating the subgenre of "practical spirituality."

Christian

If you are a Christian writer, your faith, with its theology, dogma, and strictures, is integral, not incidental, to your message. Many writers of spiritual or New Age material are practicing Christians, yet because their writing does not overtly reflect their Christian beliefs, it is not categorized in this more specific category. Readers of Christian material are generally churchgoers, and devotion to Christian teachings is paramount in their priorities.

Years ago, Christian material was confined to Christian publishers and Christian bookstores. However, today, some publishers will consider liberal Christian books if they can cross over into the mainstream market or at least into the mainstream Christian market.

Inspirational

I am not sure that even the booksellers know why there is such a separation of material called inspirational. All books, particularly spiritual books, have an inspirational component to them. These books may be presented as gifts or kept for their inspiring and uplifting content. These books may have stories of triumph over tragedy.

Inspiration is an appealing category for new spiritual writers. It looks easy. But don't be fooled. Inspirational writing makes you easy prey for the "I am the center of the universe" monster. We are all inspired by our own lives. And perhaps other people *might* be inspired by your life.

But publishers have been deluged over the years with so many "inspirational" stories that they are extremely selective. If you are highly aware of your voice and create an energy that is compelling without seeming to be all about you, you will have a better shot. This is not a contradiction. Your story is about you, but your energy needs to be about how others can be helped by what you have experienced. You need to become almost invisible.

Occult

Occult has to do with esoteric, mysterious, or supernatural spiritual practices such as tarot cards, divination, Wicca, psychic phenomena, mediumship, astrology (although astrologers would debate this), dousing, and astral projection.

Many publishers interested in spiritual or New Age material are not interested in manuscripts on occult subjects, as they feel this market is too narrow to be profitable.

Visionary Fiction

I have primarily limited my discussion of spiritual writing to nonfiction, since this comprises the vast majority of spiritual books published. However, Hal Zina Bennett—publisher, writer, editor, lecturer, and expert on this genre—has allowed me to reprint his article on the rise of what has been coined "visionary fiction."

Visionary Fiction:
Rediscovering Ancient Paths to Truth
BY HAL ZINA BENNETT

At the International New Age Trade Show in Denver several years ago, a panel of publishers, sales representatives, and booksellers agreed that it was time to establish a new book category called "visionary fiction." The reason for this was that novels appropriate to this category tended to get shelved in places where their intended readers couldn't find them. For instance, *The Celestine Prophecy* might be put in the metaphysical section but, since it is after all a novel, it might also be shelved in the literature or fantasy fiction aisles, where its intended readers were less likely to browse.

Spiritual fiction is a unique form. It's often allegorical, aimed at revealing a spiritual insight. Like the shamans' stories in ancient times, good visionary fiction takes us deep into the realm of mystery beyond the boundaries of our five senses. Here we discover truths that exist outside time and outside the finite boundaries of our singular lives. Here we encounter universal wisdom that lets us see beyond our own conflicts and passions, raising our hope that we might transcend our limited perceptions, if only momentarily, and find comfort in greater truths.

The best characters in these new novels serve as mediators between the physical world we're most familiar with and the less familiar world of dreamtime—what C. G. Jung called the "collective consciousness." These characters and lessons teach us to focus our attention on wisdom that lies outside the perceptions of our five senses or analytical minds. This allows us access to concepts that we might otherwise find just too elusive to wrap our minds around. For a short time spiritual fiction lets us look through our inner eyes and listen with our inner ears.

As an author as well as a reader of spiritual fiction, I am reminded of how important it is for us to explore and get to know the invisible reality. Love, fear, self-esteem, our sense of awe with the life force, the emotional bonds we experience with our families—all these are invisible but inseparable from everyday life. The mystery of life itself, the mystery of love, of the purpose of the cycles of life, death and rebirth—these and more challenge us. But the magic of the well-executed spiritual story helps us move beyond consensual reality and touch more enduring truths.

Like a shaman's stories of the spirit world, where the spirits of animals, trees, sky, or the stars teach us how to live, visionary fiction introduces us to a reality beyond physical reality. They often carry us deep into a consciousness once thought to be the exclusive domain of seers, visionaries, oracles, and psychics. The magic of this genre is the magic of human consciousness itself, our ability to see beneath the surface and create new visions of what our lives can be.

Contemporary society has lost touch with the deeper purpose of storytelling. The ancient teachers spun tales that allowed us to experience larger truths beyond the projections of our time-bound egos.

The best visionary fiction reaches out, urging us to pursue the mysteries of life more deeply—to bask in them. At their best, these novelists teach us how to be visionaries, reawakening an enterprise that has been the cornerstone of religions and spiritual practices the world over. Visionary fiction at its best helps us transcend the limits of our egos and experience truths beyond them. These books and their authors can help us restore forgotten relationships with the spiritual realm that we have all but lost in the busy-ness of contemporary life.

Humanity cannot truly move forward unless our collective dream is based on spiritual truths. Borrowing from the ancient teachers, this new genre offers us opportunities for contributing to a global community of visionaries who hold a dream that has been restlessly waiting to be realized since life first emerged from the cosmic mists.

Hal Zina Bennett is the author of more than thirty books on personal and spiritual development, including Write from the Heart: Unleashing the Power of Your Creativity. *He teaches seminars on writing, creativity, and shamanism throughout the United States. For more information, see* www.HalZinaBennett.com.

Publishers' Guidelines

You need a sense of what genre you belong in, not only to find your voice but also to ensure that your work reflects the appropriate protocol and style your genre requires and to determine which agents or publishers might be interested in your work. Use the lists at the back of this book as a starting place. Study books in bookstores to determine which genre your work would most likely fit into if it were turned into a book, and then note which publishers publish those books. Get their Web and mailing addresses from the copyright pages. These are your best leads for potential places to submit your manuscript. Write to them to request their manuscript-submission guidelines, including, of course, your self-addressed, stamped envelope (SASE).

Publishers' guidelines are a gold mine of information for the aspiring writer. I recommend, even if you are submitting your work to only a few publishers, to peruse the guidelines from many different houses. Some offer incredible detail about the elements of a great proposal; others—perhaps the house you are aiming for—offer little more than a few paragraphs of direction. Most can be downloaded off the publishers' Web sites.

Here are the guidelines for Beyond Words Publishing, the publisher of this book. Note the request for specific details about your manuscript, most of which hinge on your having a strong sense of the book's audience and marketing niche. Beyond Words also sends a cover letter with these guidelines that explains the company mission, scope of the list, what types of manuscripts are accepted, and how long the writer can expect to wait for a response. Since Beyond Words publishes children's fiction and nonfiction in addition to adult nonfiction, the guidelines specify the ways different material should be submitted.

Submission Guidelines

Note that we accept no e-mail submissions. Please indicate on your envelope whether your manuscript is for the adult or children's department. *All submissions should include:*

1. *A cover or query letter, with the following information:*
   - *A clear, concise description of your book.* Is it fiction or nonfiction? (Note: Our adult department publishes nonfiction only.) Who is the intended market: children, preteens, teens, adults, parents, women, etc.? Where would it be shelved in a bookstore: self-help, inspiration, women's studies, parenting, or another area? What is the approximate word count?
   - *The purpose of the book.* What is your vision for it? How will it benefit the reader? Can you distill the essence of the book and how it is unique and necessary into a few key phrases that could be used as back jacket copy, for example, or to pitch the book to booksellers?
   - *Your motivation and qualifications for writing this book.* What inspired you? What in your professional or personal experience

qualifies you to write on the subject? Why will readers want to read this book?

- *Information about your credentials as an author.* What else have you written? (Note that we publish many first-time authors, so having previously published work is not a prerequisite.)
- *Indicate whether it is a multiple submission.*

2. *A market analysis that provides:*
   - *The names, authors, and publishers of similar books on the market.* Check Bowker's *Books in Print* at your local library. You need only list books that are less than ten years old and still in print.
   - *A detailed discussion of how your proposed book differs from the competitive titles.*
   - *Sales information.* Note any best-seller lists, ranks, or awards. Check Amazon.com to determine sales rank for each book. (Note: This rank is just a snapshot of a book's rank on any given day.) Refer to the book's copyright page to get the number of times it has been reprinted.
   - *Research on potential alternative markets for the book.* What places, besides retail booksellers, could your book be sold to? We sell our books to gift stores, catalogs, museums, and book clubs; to corporate clients and the U.S. government; and translations to overseas markets. What catalogs or book clubs carry books in the same genre? Are you a member of any organization through which the book could be marketed? Are you an acknowledged expert who is asked for advice or who leads seminars at which you could market the book or use it as a program or resource material?
   - *The skills and resources you could bring to collaboratively market your book with us.* Where and how would you feel most comfortable

promoting your work? How much time could you devote to publicity? What media experience do you have? What contacts could you use to market your book? We look for authors who have a continuing commitment to market their book, long after our in-house marketing team has moved on to the next season's new titles.

3. *A proposed table of contents and detailed outline of the book.*

4. *Two to three sample chapters or full picture-book manuscript, double-spaced, on plain paper.*

5. *A self-addressed, stamped envelope (SASE)* with sufficient postage to either return your entire proposal and manuscript or for us to simply send a one-page letter reply. We cannot return your work without sufficient postage.

Please do not send us the only copy of your work. Beyond Words is not responsible for lost or misdirected manuscripts, photos, or artwork.

6

CAN SPIRIT BE CONTAINED IN AN OUTLINE?

In addition to helping you organize your thoughts so readers will be able to understand them more easily, another important reason for an outline is to enable you to see where to begin and how far you can go with your hook. Do you have enough material for a book—or only enough for a short piece like a magazine article? As an agent, I receive many manuscripts with interesting hooks, but as I read on, I notice that the author restates the same idea over and over with slight variations in the language. That's a manuscript that should have been a magazine article. If the author had outlined, he would have realized that he was not presenting fresh ideas in each chapter.

The Myth of the Outline

Writers tend to be perfectionists. We sometimes can't begin an outline because we do not have a feel for the "best" way to narrow things down.

In your high-school English class, you were probably taught how to outline. For many of us, it was the antithesis of creativity. It's easy for creative people to view outlines as contrived and tedious things that inhibit artistic impulses; we may feel that by committing to a structure, we straightjacket the natural growth of our message. On the contrary, without an outline, essentially, you ensure that your writing will grow wild. You may write, and parts of it may be brilliant, but it probably won't move forward in a purposeful direction.

Unfocused creativity is just like unharnessed electricity—it exists but has no grounding. Unlike high-school English, when you had to outline on an assigned topic, now, because you are passionate about what you want to write, an outline can flow logically out of your ideas, leaving plenty of room for inspiration and creativity along the way. It is simply a structural skeleton.

An Outline Creates a Path for You and Your Reader

An outline helps you identify the path you want your reader to follow. If you do not have a logical path, you will not sustain her interest and, therefore, not convey the information as you intend.

Spirit links you to your creativity, but your intellect must usually partner with it to create balance. The purpose of using extensive outlining techniques is to make the book feel to the reader like it was easy, like the material flowed from a place of passion and logic, easily and purely. A good outline gives no hint of the writer's angst!

An Outline Gives Birth to Your Table of Contents

Unless you are writing a scholarly book, you do not need innumerable categories and subcategories. Let's look at the mechanics of an outline, which, as you'll see, can essentially be recast to make up your book's table of contents. The primary topics of your outline are your chapters; subtopics are the elements within the chapter that will enable you to create a logical whole; sometimes they will be called out as actual subheads within your book, sometimes not.

The table of contents is the tree trunk from which all chapter limbs will extend. When I first start writing, I often think I can begin writing with the branches, ignoring the limbs and the tree trunk itself. I then discover I am "out of my tree." Bad joke aside, your table of contents will follow the logic and chronology of your outline.

Begin by introducing your thesis, either in chapter 1, or literally in an introduction. Subsequent chapters will elaborate on specific aspects of your thesis. Subheadings within those chapters will get even more detailed; when you get to the editing stage, these can be a handy way to check that you haven't strayed from your topic. The last chapter should summarize—that is, briefly restate your thesis and the contents of the chapters—and then conclude, perhaps by inviting the reader to use this information to go forward incorporating your message into his own life.

Below is a sample outline that illustrates some of these points. Suppose the hook is this: "Office meditation enhances your productivity, job satisfaction, and feelings of control over your work environment. This book gives you a humorous and inspiring guide to creating moments of intimate personal space and a communion with the rhythms of the day even within an impersonal and hectic office."

1. Introduction: Set the stage for the book's premise by noting the stress and hectic pace of modern office life, a pace that is not conducive to reflection or feeling in control.
2. Chapter 1: Meditation as a Tool
   2.1. Draw the reader into the book with a compelling scene: An important client is about to abandon the company because of their latest interaction with you. You've been called into an emergency meeting.
      2.1.1. Without meditation: Describe the scene, your composure, and others' reactions to you in the meeting.

      2.1.2. With meditation: Describe the scene, your composure, and others' reactions to you in the meeting.

  2.2 Summarize the benefits of office meditation and invite the reader to learn more in the rest of the book. Introduce some simple relaxation techniques easily used in everyday life.

3. Chapter 2: Meditation breaks

Analyze the typical work day as having six opportunities to reconnect with the earth's rhythms and put your workday stresses into perspective:

  3.1. In the morning, in your car, before you go into the office, as a way to center yourself and set an intention for the upcoming day.

  3.2. After you greet your co-workers and sit down to your desk, in reflection of their gifts and your place in the office community.

  3.3. Midmorning, as you do a stretching routine or take a walk to refresh your mind and perspective by looking at the world around you.

  3.4. Before you eat lunch, as a thankfulness reflection on the bounty of your life.

  3.5. Midafternoon, as you appreciate the fatigue and sense of accomplishment of a job well done.

  3.6. At day's end, as you reflect and offer thanks for another day of life and your ability to contribute to it.

4. Chapters 3–7:

Specific office problems: co-worker hassles, a task that seems too difficult, a deadline, a boss whom you dislike, support staff who are not supportive, etc. Each chapter elaborates on its specific situation with exercises, examples from interviews, and easy-to-follow practices.

5. Summary and conclusion.

Outlining Chapters

Outlining is once again a time when it's useful to know your genre. Look at the typical chapter count of books comparable to yours. (Many spiritual nonfiction books seem to be around ten to twelve chapters long.) Then write the appropriate number of possible chapter headings on index cards or list them in your word processor's outline feature. At this point you might only be working with topics rather than specific chapter titles. If you do invent some titles, make sure they clearly reflect the content you want to convey. Once you have your labels, move the cards or text around until the order of the chapters makes sense.

Though the chapters should flow in a logical order (determined by your hook), also keep in mind that each one should be able to stand alone. If a chapter is dependent on the previous chapter in order to make sense, it probably does not warrant being separate. Of course, books are typically meant to be read sequentially, and each chapter builds on the previous ones, but each chapter should be a freestanding unit with a thesis, introductory statement or statements, support for your ideas, and a conclusion that summarizes and then leads the reader to the topic of the next chapter.

For each chapter, elaborate on its topic with as many subtopics as a reader would need to understand the full message you want to convey. If you're doing this manually, put one subtopic on a card and then lay these subtopic cards in line below the card for that chapter. Proceed until you're satisfied that you've created enough detail for each chapter. *Hint:* This is called brainstorming! It's not so hard; in fact, it's fun. Write down your first thoughts, don't edit as you go, and work fast, letting the spirit flow. Later, when the spirit has cooled and you can look at your outline with a cold eye, type it up. Does it still make sense? Do all your subtopics really relate to that chapter, or are some better suited elsewhere in the book? Do you have a thesis for each chapter, and is each one supported?

Writers can become intimidated when they consider the daunting task of turning this stack of index cards into a book. Don't be. Chapters of a book are like any other good writing: They have a beginning, a middle, and an end. In fact, each paragraph has a beginning, a middle, and an end. Simple as it sounds, some writers have to struggle with this concept, and the result is confused writing that is difficult for readers to follow. So, be sure everything you write follows this logical order: *beginning; middle; end*. Viewed this way, you can see that even an overwhelming amount of information can be broken down into manageable bites. Take each chapter of the book as a small bite.

Chapter length varies from book to book. The trend in publishing today is toward shorter chapters and paragraphs, based on the assumption that people are busy and have a great deal of competition for their leisure time. A shorter book with individual chapters that can be digested in a single sitting accommodates that assumption.

When you compile your outline, you develop a sense of how long your book needs to be. A page count for a standard six-by-nine-inch book is approximately 250 pages. A fairly standard page length for a nonfiction book would be about 200 words, which is about the equivalent of a 50,000-word manuscript. If you divide your book into ten chapters, then you know you will have approximately 5,000 words per chapter. Keep in mind that manuscript page length varies considerably from published-book page length. If you want to keep the chapters shorter for visual appeal and simplification of format, add more chapters and narrow the focus of each.

Publishers and Agents Will Read Your Table of Contents

A good message can get lost in poorly organized writing. Agents and publishers want a manuscript without tiresome digressions. Think about an excited child who tries to tell a story. You hear all kinds of extraneous details that might be interesting but take you away from the main point. There is more latitude in verbal effusiveness than there is in the written word. When you are bubbling over about something in a conversation, most of your digressions will add color. In writing, they are simply annoying.

Spiritual writing is not about the writer, it is about the message. Outlining allows our logical, ordering intellect to work with our effusive, enthusiastic spirit so we can capture truth—a universal energy—within this limited form of communication. When we do this successfully, our work can be understood by even the uninitiated reader. Organizing your message is the best way to avoid writing with an obtuseness that some might interpret as condescension. It prevents you from alienating readers who are striving and searching. If you make it easy for readers to follow your ideas, you remove one more barrier to their understanding and to their moving forward on their own path. If you can create order out of spirit, you are truly a co-creator with the divine. No one can teach you talent, creativity, or God-connection. But you can certainly learn to write a good outline.

7

WRITING AND EDITING

After you've outlined your book, the next step is to put some flesh on that skeleton. It is time to write. Some people liken writing and publishing a book to birthing a baby: some groaning, some pain, a lot of excitement, and a great reward at the end. And you have all the skills and preparation you need to birth this babe. Remember, your book already exists at some level. You are able to write it as only you can. It is your spirit waiting to manifest itself in words. People will read it and love it. This should make you feel good. But I am a writer, so I know it may not. It might even make you nervous and doubt yourself even more than when you had no idea of how to write a book.

The Sacred Act of Writing

You write. Sometimes it flows, fast and furious. Other times each word has to be wrenched out of you, but you write, write, write, until you are exhausted or finished, whichever comes first.

Have you ever finished a project, and when you finally sit back and read it you almost can't believe it came from you? You know you were there. You know you feel exhausted and blissful. You may even have a flare-up of carpal tunnel syndrome. But when the writing is finished, you also have a sense of awe that you were ever intelligent or wise enough to have written it at all. The product may need refining, but if you are blessed to experience the deep connection of spiritual writing, you recognize how spirit has taken you to a place beyond intellect and into the world of creation.

It takes a certain level of faith to allow oneself to be lost in the process of writing. Humans have developed intellects that tell us there is something inherently unsafe or frightening about suspending time and space. Writing isn't for the fainthearted. It takes practice and a certain level of intimacy with your soul to reach a state of writing bliss. But with trust and patience, anyone who truly wants to write can do so.

When you are ready to really get into your writing, the first step is to discover which circumstances and environment most effectively allow you to journey inward on your creative quest. Some people like to write in silence. Some people like to have music blaring. As I am sure you have determined, or soon will, there is no one correct way. The only rule is this: No matter where you choose to write, look closely at yourself until you find the optimal way to maintain a sacred space within yourself as you work.

As you determine what is optimum, also try to determine what is minimum. If you want to be a writer as more than a once-in-a-millennium hobby, learn how to accommodate your needs with a measure of flexibility. Experiment with different situations to isolate what it is that makes you more productive on certain occasions than others. For example, I have figured out that I need to be in some kind of closed space with a clean desk. If I work in my office at home, I don't care if my children come in screaming at the top of their lungs or if the entire room is cluttered to the ceiling; if my desk is clear and the door is shut, I'm fine.

Many writers also find that they can write well only for a particular length of time. When the well runs dry for me after two or three hours, I need to take a break. That is why I am always juggling several little projects at once. Some people, like my husband, think it is because I have an attention span the size of a piece of macaroni, but really I am just priming the pump.

Now that you've understood the essential role the outline can play in helping you envision the shape of your book, let it go. At this stage, the outline is a basic road map—but spirit is your tour guide. Writing from your outline does not have to be linear; don't avoid unexpected detours in favor of finding the shortest distance to your destination. Though you will eventually pare down your text and make sure every word relates to your thesis so the end product is well organized, don't hold too tightly to your outline during the initial writing process or you might miss some exciting adventures that you haven't anticipated. This may not be easy at first, but it will be vastly rewarding.

When you have found the best way to reach your sacred writing space, use your outline to guide you back to the main road after any digressions or side tours. Without your map you might find yourself driving around in circles. However, sometimes writers are surprised to find that a detour moves them into an altogether unexpected direction. Don't resist the possibility that your book wants to move you toward an even better perspective than the one you have anticipated. Your book is alive, after all.

Once the outline is written and the manuscript has been envisioned by your creative source and the divine voice, it already exists. Your job is then to capture it and give it form. Guidance can be mistaken for control. Just as with raising a child, remember that he or she has a separate path and that the more control you impose the more resistance you will receive. By allowing some space, you encourage growth, so don't edit yourself at this stage or try to control your inner voice. You can go back and refine the limits you hope to set, but avoid squeezing your writing so hard that it can't breathe. If you find that you have extraneous ideas or concepts that don't fit anywhere within your current piece, write them down in another notebook or computer document. Later, you can patch them together or perhaps find you have the makings for another project.

When you let your ideas flow onto paper, don't look ahead to how many words you need to make it a book. Write as much as you feel you can in one sitting and then forget about it. Live your life. Don't pressure yourself to produce a certain amount of material per day. If you write until your spirit says you are finished, you will find that you have a book much sooner than if you keep checking your word count to see if you are done.

Modern life makes many demands on our time, and many of us are trying to start writing careers while still emotionally and financially supporting ourselves and our families. When at all possible, carve out a time and place that is inviolable. You may need to sacrifice something or carefully negotiate to eke out a space, but it is part of the job. Some writers will keep their books hidden in their desk drawers so they can tackle them during lunch and breaks; some write during the short window after their children fall asleep and before they themselves do. Writers who must "steal" time to write may keep a journal with them so they can keep creative thoughts fresh until they find a better time to really give them life. Do whatever works. Finding time to answer your inner calling to write is not optional; it is a requirement for your spiritual well-being. Not everyone may write material that will ultimately be published, but anyone can tap into his inner voice to become a divine writer.

The Values—and Perils—of Feedback

Once you've written a good chunk of text, but well before you finish the book, it's time to gain some perspective on your work. Seeking and receiving others' feedback is integral to the writing process. It takes great courage to expose your intimate thoughts and hard work to criticism, but this step carries you further toward becoming a professional writer who recognizes how the editing process strengthens your work.

Perhaps the best way to get useful feedback about your writing is to find objective readers—people whose judgment or intellect you respect—and ask them to read and comment on your work-in-progress. You're not asking them to edit or proofread the book for you; it's far too early for that. What you are looking for are impressions and global recommendations for changes in content or tone. Here are some questions to pose to your readers in order to maximize the value of their feedback:

1. Is the subject interesting to them and addressed in sufficient detail?
2. Does anything distract them as they read: redundancies; digressions; too much author presence; a tone that doesn't match the subject matter or that is too preachy or didactic?
3. What do they like best about the piece? Why?
4. Is it easy to comprehend, or are there gaps where transitions or explanations are needed?
5. What questions does reading it raise in their minds?
6. Does the manuscript seem to carry through on what it promises at the outset? Do they feel that you have said what you mean to say?

When choosing readers, try to match them to the subject matter. Envision your book's audience and find a person who fits that profile. For example, if you're writing about the laying on of hands, with supportive anecdotes of faith healing, a left-brain, "where's the scientific evidence" engineer type of reader may not be the best choice; after all, he or she is probably not the target audience for your book.

Another great way to find support is by joining or forming a writing group or attending a writers' conference or workshop. Though it can be intimidating, writing groups have an advantage over simply showing your work to nonwriters—namely, you aren't always in the hot seat. Accepting criticism can be tiring, and in a group setting you have opportunities to critique others' work, which can have the added benefit of giving you greater insights into your own. Also, writers who know that their own work will be scrutinized next can often find more creatively constructive ways of pointing out weak areas in others' writing.

Keep in mind that all opinions are subjective and when several people are involved, such as in a writing group, the dynamics of a particular group can be a blessing or a curse. Ideally, your most significant strengths or weaknesses will be identified by several people making similar comments, or you will get a range of responses that will show you how the same work can affect different readers. Unfortunately, in some groups, decorum can take precedence over candor and you'll get no more illuminating feedback than "That is so great; I loved it." Others can become a cauldron of jealousy, with one person's good writing seen as a threat to the others. In groups like that, praise is either given grudgingly or wrapped within a cutting critique.

It takes time to figure out who are your best critics. Seek people who share your passions, whose writing is at the same level or better, who have a healthy sense of self-respect, and who admire you for your accomplishments. They will neither be afraid to critique or to praise. When you have a friend whose comments you trust completely and whose edits make your words sing, you have found gold!

When you do hear negative or constructive comments, try not to give in to feelings of being personally violated. Don't cling to your specific words as if they are a reflection of your worth. That is the mark of an inexperienced writer. Learning to accept criticism gracefully and to discuss differences of opinion will help you gain more insight into your writing and how other people might receive your message. You need this objectivity—it's impossible to achieve the same results alone. Confronted with perspectives you may have never considered, you will find new ways to enhance your work, or you may recognize an area that needs more development.

Keep in mind, however, that if you show your manuscript to ten different people, even if every one of them has your best interests at heart, you will get ten different opinions—maybe even some that directly contradict each other. Listen courteously—you did invite comment, after all!—but remember that ultimately the work is yours and you will decide on the final form. This is a true test for the "people pleaser" within many of us and a case where a strong sense of self and confidence in your message is vital.

One of the primary values of feedback is that you see your work through others' eyes and glaring errors in tone or holes in content leap forward. You'll gain a fresh perspective and a sense of renewal after you've sought feedback and gleaned the best from each reader. And that's a good thing, because assimilating that feedback leads to the next stage in the process: editing.

Even Spirit Needs an Editor

When you write, the creative process is not bound by the standards of time and space, nor should it be. Creativity demands an unfettered mind. Only when the mind is free, with no heed to the inner critic, can your true voice emerge.

But now that your spiritual voice has emerged, it's exuberant, it's enthusiastic—and it needs to be edited! After getting feedback from others and perhaps by rereading your own words with a cold eye, you've found that, hard as it is to believe, this product of spirit needs to be refined. When you are in the throes of writing ecstasy, the words often soar, even bringing you to laughter or tears as you read your words expressing what is in your heart. It is difficult at this stage to imagine that your writing is imperfect.

After the flow has ebbed, writers often forget—or haven't yet learned—the need for collaborative effort, and they will try to own the words. So, it is important that after you write you allow your words to leave the confines of your mind and the safety of your soul. You put them—and yourself—out there where everyone can see. When enough time has elapsed that you are able to read your words without your ego looking over your shoulder, you can go back to your manuscript and self-edit.

Self-Editing

Self-editing is when you hold a red pencil in your hand and look at something you have written with total disdain. You take that red pencil and scribble all over your writing, "This stinks!" You crumple it up and toss it into the fireplace. Well, that's not actually self-editing. That's me after a first draft.

Conceptual Editing

True editing has two different levels. The first is conceptual editing. This is when you look at your manuscript to see how well the words convey what you wish to say. When you look at a manuscript conceptually, you see both what is there and what is *not* there. Writers often believe that everything they wish to convey is present on the page because it exists in their brain. When you reread your own words, your brain fills in the gaps in the concepts even if they are not completely clear to anyone else. This lack of transitions, or of connecting and elaborating thoughts between ideas, is common to anyone who writes with fervor. It is an easily remedied problem, but it takes a fresh eye to see what is not there. You cannot possibly edit conceptually until you've let your manuscript sit for days or even weeks.

Another element of conceptual editing is analyzing a manuscript for what there is *too much* of. A common mistake of writers is to rephrase and reemphasize key points, because they are so important. That is what we

82

do in oral speech: we reiterate, restate, and emphasize to make our point. The audience doesn't mind the repetition, presumably because the speaker is there to engage them on other levels: facial expressions, hand gestures, bodily movement, and even props. But you are neither teaching nor giving a speech. Repeating important ideas in your manuscript because they are *"so important"* is irritating to readers. And you will probably do it—most of us do.

Sometimes when a project is just finished, the prospect of reading it in its entirety is simply too tiring. Skipping this important step, however, will cause you to miss the places where you have rambled or unintentionally repeated yourself. When you are writing chapter after chapter of a long manuscript, especially when you have a strong thesis, it is natural for ideas to get repeated. You won't be able to tell if you've repeated too much until you've given yourself time to recharge so you have the energy to read it all the way through.

If a reader wants to reread your key concepts, that is his prerogative. But by forcing him to reread what he has already read, it will appear that you underestimate his intelligence, believing he may not be able to understand the importance of the message the first time—or the second, or the third. Few people will purposefully pay to be insulted or bored. So when you edit, cut redundancies and imperative language ("you must," "you should," etc.). Avoid, as much as possible, the use of "I." This is your book, and you are integral in it, but too much "I" leaves little room for the reader's "you" and makes the book seem self-indulgent and amateurish.

Line Editing

The second level of editing is line editing, in which you look at your manuscript, line by line, for errors in grammar, spelling, and punctuation. Study the individual words. Are they necessary or redundant? Strive for tight writing. This means

- Cutting words that do not serve a purpose
- Avoiding digressions that do not relate back to your outline
- Eliminating flowery language that is there simply for its floweriness
- Not being too impressed with your own cleverness
- Reducing the pomposity of grandiose statements that are unsupported or do not lead to reasonable and logical conclusions
- Releasing the bondage of overly tortured prose before you exhaust your reader
- Getting to the point before you lose your reader altogether
- Keeping paragraphs short

After you have tightened up any wordiness, check your grammar. Do your subjects agree with their predicates? Have you spelled all proper names correctly? You do not need to have the skills of a copy editor or proofreader, but you will naturally want your manuscript to be free of obvious grammatical and spelling errors. Refer to *The Chicago Manual of Style* (the stylebook used by most publishers) if you have any questions. Strunk and White's *Elements of Style* is widely regarded as the definitive resource on basic writing technique and provides an excellent discussion of many common grammatical problems.

A note of caution about word-processor grammar and spell checkers: They make mistakes. They are not proofreaders. If you change everything without looking at each suggested change, item by item, you will wind up with a very strange manuscript.

Lastly, before you submit your manuscript, format it so that it is double-spaced, single-sided, with page numbers, uniform margins of at least one inch on all sides, uniform chapter heads and subheads, and chapter titles that agree with your table of contents. Refer to the publisher's guidelines for specific directives, and follow them. It's like putting on your best clothes for a job interview; little details make a good impression.

Outside Editing

When you reach a point when you have exhausted all of the standard methods of self-editing, you might want to find an objective person to give you a more in-depth read than your earlier readers provided. The key word is *objective*—not someone who is your constant cheerleader, not someone who has no critical skills, and not someone who may be grinding his own writer's axe and critiquing you too harshly.

It is also best if you find someone to edit your manuscript who does not have any stake in where you sleep at night (*code*: not your spouse!). Be aware that not everyone is supportive and that not everyone is right about everything. Again, as with your readers, take in what people say, but take it with a grain of salt. If you find something useful, you can incorporate it. If the critique turns up something which shows you that the reader has no clue what you are doing, it doesn't mean the person is a dunce. It might be a flag that you have not made yourself completely clear.

If you can find a supportive person who is intelligent, blunt, and interested in your success to edit your manuscript, you are truly blessed. My best friend, Dawn, is such a person, and I would also trust her to pick out clothing and husbands. She doesn't sugarcoat a thing, and I love her for it.

What Do Agents and Editors Say about Editing?

The answer to this question is simple: Thank you for editing your work. When you hand in a well-edited manuscript you save so much energy on the part of the agent or editor. It is easier for them to make an informed decision on whether to acquire a manuscript when they don't have to deal with the distractions of content and stylistic errors.

Editors and agents look for submissions that have already been tweaked. A clean manuscript is just one more check mark in the plus column for you. It will have good and consistent transitions from one thought and one paragraph to the next. The chapters will follow logically, without extraneous and random sentences that don't seem to belong anywhere or glaring redundancies. How logically and completely that content is organized and how professionally and attractively it is presented on paper all have an impact on a publisher's confidence in you, the likelihood of an offer, and the advance you might receive.

As a first-time author, don't submit a manuscript to a publisher expecting that if they like it well enough they will assign someone to edit it. Publishing houses are typically understaffed. They are looking for books that will have the most sales potential and that will require the least amount of in-house resources. Every dollar spent on editing an incomplete manuscript cuts into their profit margin. You want your submission to be as pristine as you can possibly make it. Taking the effort to exceed a publisher's expectations can only help you fullfill your mission. In other words, make sure your manuscript or proposal is absolutely ready to be made public, that it is the best version you can possibly achieve, and that it adheres to the industry's guidelines before you bother sending it out. Do not look for second chances.

Part Three
FROM MANUSCRIPT TO PUBLICATION

When you are satisfied that your manuscript is the best it can be, it's time to send it out into the world. Cynthia Black and I have gathered information from all aspects of the publishing community; in the next chapters, you'll learn who the players are in the publishing industry, how to prepare your entrée into it by way of your query and book proposal, and what happens when an agent or publisher is interested in your work.

As you know, nothing is guaranteed. You are not a failure if you do not reach publication. Not everyone will, because not everyone is meant to be published. Try not to become so determined to control the outcome that you forget to see the lessons along the way. There may be other, unseen reasons for your efforts.

On the other hand, although you do not want to be so stiff-necked as to miss inner guidance, you do not want, at this point, to even think of not reaching your goal. Give your work your best intentions. When you have done that, turn it over to the universe. If you open to your spirit, you will know what path to take. You'll give wings to your writing when you learn how to use the protocols of publishing to your best advantage. So, engage your left brain—the part of you that is not pure spirit bursting forth with creativity—and turn the page.

8

THE PUBLISHING HOUSE

When you get an offer to publish your book, you'll deal with many, many people along the publishing pipeline as well as with changes to your text, title, and perhaps even your concept. These changes will start at the macro level—your angle and the book's overall tone and content—and move in a progressively micro direction. Each person who assists you takes a more detailed look at what you have written. Let's look at the players in the process, some of whom you may never see or speak with (like the publisher), others of whom you will work with closely (like the managing editor). Before we do, however, there are two other concepts that are essential to understanding the way a publishing house works: the imprint and the list.

The Imprint

A publishing house often publishes materials under what is called an imprint. Some houses have only one, others many. Imprints are ways of organizing the "personalities" of a house. For example, a large house might have a business imprint, a religious imprint, and a children's imprint. Or it might break it up even further, with one children's imprint for hardcover books and another for a lighter original paperback series. Occasionally editors who have outstanding financial success with their books are granted their own imprints, usually with their name attached.

The endless variety of imprints is yet another reason why your preliminary research is essential to your success as a writer; if you don't know the scope of the imprint to which you are sending your manuscript, you are probably wasting everyone's time—not to mention throwing away the money you spend on postage.

The List

A list is a publishing house's collection of books published, and it is further refined as the "frontlist" and "backlist" to distinguish new titles from older ones. The publishing year is divided into two or three seasons, usually fall and spring (and more recently, winter), a convention dating back to the days when publishers had to ship books by water. Nothing could be transported when the rivers were frozen, so publishers got books out in the fall, before the winter freeze, and in the spring, after the thaw.

The placement of a book in a particular season's list is often part of a marketing strategy. Gift and holiday books are published, naturally, on the fall list so they can be pushed for the holiday season, and a book on the occult might come out before Halloween. Winter books might relate to Black History month or Valentine's day. Books with a lighter feel or a summer theme might appear on the spring list, as might books that pertain to graduation, Mother's Day, Easter, or Passover.

The Publisher

The publisher views the publishing house from a global perspective, ensuring that the business end of publishing—sales, marketing, contracts, suppliers, distributors, hiring and firing—runs smoothly. While publishers are not usually involved with day-to-day editorial issues, they set the editorial tone for the house—what sort of books editors should try to acquire, what sort of markets the sales staff should target.

Publishers typically do not work with the author, except in smaller houses, where they are often involved in contract negotiations. The smaller, independent houses, with their direct publisher involvement, sometimes compensate for a smaller advance with more personal attention to you and your book. As an author, attention from your publisher means that your book is particularly important to the house, that it is not just a slot filling out a list and will merit no more publicity than a mention in a catalog. The top twelve conglomerates in the publishing industry are not your only options; there are over 55,000 independent publishers in the United States.

Independent and large publishing houses each have different general pros and cons for authors. We have highlighted some of these for you, though keep in mind that there can be a lot of variation between houses.

Large versus Independent Publishers

Because publishing has a certain glamour to it and because the fame and infamy of certain best-selling authors is so prominent, it often surprises writers to find out that, generally, publishing isn't a business that generates a lot of wealth. In the past, it was a "gentlemen's profession," invoking a respectable—and perhaps a little shabby—sense of bookishness and tradition. To this day the markup (and therefore, profit) on books is not high, and the salaries of those who work in the industry are typically far below comparable positions in other fields. As you get familiar with the industry, keep in mind that individuals who are attracted to publishing are not there to get rich but because they love books.

The main difference between large and small publishing houses, as you'll see from the following list, tends to be cash flow. But the large houses often have ready access to this money because they are owned by huge corporations that make larger profits with sister companies. This gives them the freedom to strategically pick the books they view as the best potential money-makers and concentrate promotional efforts into one big push. Other advantages and disadvantages to the large versus independent houses are as follows:

Large Publishers

Pros

- Offer prestige
- Have wider distribution
- Offer higher advances
- Have a higher budget for promotion
- Have more access to media outlets
- Get more visibility at bookseller conventions
- Improve the writer's reputation when seeking future book contracts
- Are usually located in New York City, the publishing mecca

Cons

- Tend to focus publicity on certain key titles; may not promote your book at all
- May "orphan" books due to the high turnover rate of editorial staff
- Are less inclined to develop projects
- Offer less personal involvement or concern with you and the success of your book
- Still require you to promote your own book after initial efforts at publicity
- May lose your book among all the other books on their list
- Usually take from one to two years to release books
- Are more likely to be disrupted by company mergers and acquisitions

- Typically drop titles after three years
- Destroy inventory they can't sell
- Can take months with contract and rights-reversion paperwork

Independent Publishers

Pros

- Have a more personal, emotional investment in you and the success of your book
- May offer more developmental and editing support
- Guarantee your book at least some publicity
- Are more likely to take risks on unpublished authors
- Can move quickly if a book needs to get out fast (six months)
- Are more flexible and can often grow with you
- Will take the time to sell to markets other than bookstores
- Will nourish their backlist titles, keeping books in print much longer
- May offer more generous royalties over the long term
- Sometimes are likely to do more with foreign rights

Cons

- Offer modest or no advances
- May have smaller print runs (a first printing for a small press averages 4,400, according to *The Rest of Us: The First Study of America's 53,000 Independent Smaller Book Publishers* [Book Industry Study Group, 1999])
- Have a low budget for promotion
- May have cash-flow challenges
- May have smaller distribution
- May have less experience or resources
- Are less recognized by the media and reviewers

Editors

In any given house are editors with various titles: editor in chief, editorial director, acquisitions editor, developmental editor, managing editor, copy editor. Some titles differences—editorial assistant, assistant editor, associate editor, senior editor, executive editor—merely indicate seniority among editors of the same class. In some houses the roles blend; in others they are quite distinct. Each house defines its editorial roles slightly differently.

The Editor in Chief

The editor in chief, sometimes known as the editorial director, is the editor to whom all the other editors report. Usually, she has the final editorial say, unless there are editors in the house who, because of their successful record at picking good books, are given special autonomy or their own imprint. The editor in chief decides which titles will "lead" the season's list (that is, which are the most significant and deserve the most publicity, marketing dollars, and editorial attention) and has the final say on how they will be presented (hardcover or softcover, black-and-white or color, high-quality paper or not, etc.). Her role is to see the entire list and know how to allocate resources so that every book is given the attention it merits in order to maximize revenue to the house.

Acquisitions Editors

The acquisitions editor is the person whose name you need to know when you are sending an unsolicited query letter or proposal. His primary job is to read submissions and acquire new books for the house to publish. He also looks for trends and tries to find new people, through seminars and articles, whose ideas and skills might lend themselves to a book.

Acquisitions editors, or their assistants, sift through submissions—both those that the editor may have received or solicited from agents and those from the slush pile (the stack of unsolicited manuscripts)—always hoping to find a gem. An acquisitions editor must have a good sense of what types of books work for the house and an eye for what will sell.

Before you send your query or proposal off to an acquisitions editor, read the house guidelines. Does the house accept unsolicited manuscripts or proposals, or only queries? Or does it accept only agented manuscripts?

Developmental Editors

If your book is acquired by a publishing house, you may be assigned an editor who will help you with its development. The developmental editor will look at the manuscript to determine if its content is well-structured and complete. If a developmental editor is involved before you have written a complete manuscript, you will receive invaluable tutelage that will make you a better writer overall.

Of course, the need for further development of your idea depends on the state of your manuscript and how closely aligned your vision of the topic is with the editor's vision of a marketable book on the subject. Ideally, these two visions are congruent and your book will not need further development, other than the fine-tuning of line editing and proofreading.

But if it does need development, don't be insulted. Obviously, the editor likes where you're going; she just wants to help you get there. A good developmental editor will give you a second set of objective eyes to continue with the conceptual editing you already did. Your writer's ego does not like anyone to tell you that anything needs to be changed in your manuscript. Remember that the developmental editor is your friend. But it's hard, because you have sold the book to the publisher, so you know they like it, and then they tell you it needs to be changed. It is easy to take it personally, but it's essential that you let this go and conduct yourself professionally. Editors know the publishing business;

you don't. Their comments are designed to make your good work even more marketable, so be humble and allow yourself to learn from their expertise.

It is impossible for a writer to be totally objective about his own work. Although your nerves may be raw at the first sign of red pen, get some distance, consider the suggestions, and then determine if you agree or not. Some authors claim that they have never needed to be edited. Pshaw! Even Hemingway needed to be edited!

At this point, editing is a back-and-forth process, and your input is valued. If you feel that the editor was mistaken or did not understand what you are trying to convey, let her know—and tell her why! If, for example, your editor cuts a paragraph that you think is essential, a note in the margin from you saying, "Put this back in," is not nearly as helpful as one saying, "This paragraph is important because it describes a process that will be referred to later in the book." Be as clear as possible. There is no need to be overly dramatic or antagonistic. Everyone's goal is to help you create a better book that will reach the greatest number of readers.

Managing Editors

Once a manuscript has been conceptually edited and is ready for the production process, the managing editor steps in. His role is to maintain, communicate, and enforce all phases of the editorial and production schedule. His duties include scheduling the book's production; hiring copy editors, proofreaders, designers, and artists for the book's cover and interior; sending prepublication galleys to reviewers; filing necessary forms with the Library of Congress and the copyright office; and coordinating the production process with the author, proofreader, designer, typesetter, prepress house, printer, and bindery. You will be in contact with him frequently as your book moves through the copyediting and proofreading stages.

Copy Editors and Proofreaders

Copy editors look at your manuscript, line by line, just as you did earlier. But they are experts. The copy editor will look for how clearly your message is conveyed, on a sentence-by-sentence basis, and will note errors in grammar, conventions, spelling, and punctuation. The copy editor will fact-check any quotations or proper names. She will also tighten up your writing, removing extraneous words and phrases. Some copy editors work with electronic copy; others still mark up manuscripts the old-fashioned way with red pen and flagged queries to you. Most book publishers use *The Chicago Manual of Style* to ensure that all their books are consistent. Some houses develop their own stylebook, and it is the copy editor's job to ensure that these styles are adhered to. The copy editor will also mark the various design elements within a manuscript (such as bulleted lists and levels of headings) for the designer to use to create the interior template for your book.

Once a manuscript is copyedited, it goes back to the author to review the marks and answer the copy editor's queries, which are specific questions about the manuscript. Copy editors query the author for consistency, accuracy, and clarity. You may be asked to verify a source, change language that is incompatible with the house mission, or clarify whether the "Richard" on page 33 should actually be "William" as on the previous page. Many questions will need a simple "yes" or "no" answer, but some queries require an explanation on your part. Again, avoid answering detailed questions with "Don't worry about it" or "OK, whatever." This is not particularly helpful to the copy editor. Be clear and concise.

After a manuscript has been copyedited, it is sent to a proofreader, who scrutinizes every word and punctuation mark for possible typos, misspellings, and grammatical errors. There is no conceptual editing whatsoever at this stage. The proofreader looks for mechanical flaws. The text is then translated from manuscript to galley form, which means your work is reset with the typeface and page layout it will later have in the bound book. After the manuscript has been laid out, it will be proofread again, this time for layout errors, and it will also be reviewed by the author.

When a writer is given the galley proofs, the expectation is that no further changes will be made in the manuscript. If libelous or embarrassing mistakes are found, of course they can be changed, but at this stage any changes are expensive and prohibitive and will likely delay a book's publication date, which will have a negative impact on sales and publicity plans, most of which are arranged up to six months prior to the publication date. The copy editor will also review the "bluelines." These are equivalent to contact prints of film negatives that show precisely how your work will appear in its final form. Except in cases of extreme errors, bluelines are reviewed primarily for confirmation, as changes at this stage are excessively costly.

Sales and Marketing

The sales staff at a publishing house or its distributor are major players in the overall success of your book. Members of the house sales staff attend editorial meetings when potential acquisitions are discussed, and if they do not see the market potential in a book, it can be shot down right then.

Each publisher has a limited number of "frontlist" books, those books that are new each season, and they want to make sure the books chosen have the most commercial potential. They also want books that "pull" the backlist along. This means they look for new titles that complement and can be marketed alongside older titles that need a little extra help moving off the shelf.

A sales force who is excited about your book will directly affect the number of copies retailers order. That's why, at every step of the way— and especially with your proposal—you want to present a high-quality product that shows you are thinking of your book in terms of its marketability. When you are persuading an editor to buy your book, remember you are also trying to persuade the sales staff, who will later be trying to persuade the buyers at the bookstore chains and independent booksellers. Marketers, being more business- than editorial-oriented, need to see your book's market potential even more than an editor who may be more swayed by high-quality prose.

So when you've narrowed down the publishers to whom you'll submit, research which markets they sell to. Is it to bookstores only? Or do they sell to libraries, catalogues, book clubs, corporations, schools, gift shops, or discount clubs? Do they sell to the secular market (i.e., mainstream books), or to the Christian Booksellers Association stores, or to New Age bookstores? What is their distribution method? How many sales reps are selling for them? Do they have sales reps call on the chain bookstores like Barnes & Noble, Borders, or Walden? What has been their success rate with a book like yours?

Getting this kind of information takes some sleuthing. First, get the publisher's catalog and read their Web site. Research on the Web or at the library for magazine articles about the publisher and their business practices. *Publishers Weekly* and the *NAPRA ReView* magazines often profile individual publishers and their books. Bookstore Web sites and magazines that carry spiritual material, such as the Bodhi Tree Bookstore and the *Ruminator Review*, will show you which books work for them. Any information you can glean to show how your book will appeal to the individual markets listed above will help you craft a proposal that will appeal to the house marketing staff.

Publicity

All publishers have some form of in-house publicity. What you may find surprising is that you may have more publicity effort on your behalf from smaller houses than you will from larger houses. Large publishing houses typically acquire a few major (*code*: a large, six- to seven-figure author advance) books per season and devote a great deal of their publicity budget to those megahit books. They also have "mid-list" books that do not receive much attention or publicity dollars but which fill out their seasonal offerings. While the houses will perform some perfunctory publicity efforts for these mid-list books, their focus is elsewhere. Large houses will expect authors to do a lot in the way of their own publicity.

Independent publishing houses acquire fewer titles and do not have such an obvious split between "important" books and books that fill out the list. Not every book can lead the list, but the smaller houses invest more into the publicity and success of all their books because each book has a greater proportional impact on the financial health of the publisher than at the larger houses. However, because they are smaller, these houses still expect your full partnership and participation in seeking publicity for your own book.

In chapter 11, "The Book Proposal," we'll look in greater detail at how you can strengthen your ability to publicize your book.

9

AGENTS

Do I Need an Agent?

As both agented and independent writers get published, the answer to this question really depends on what sort of publishing path you want to take: A large or independent house? What kind of advance? After reading this chapter you should be able to make an informed decision on your own.

A literary agent's job is to screen and find manuscripts to sell to publishers. Acting as a writer's business representative, an agent who agrees to represent you will review your work, advise you about its quality and market potential, and devise a strategy to pitch it to publishers who he thinks will be the most interested in your work. If a publisher then makes you an offer, the agent will negotiate contract terms for you.

To some extent, agents have become the publishing world's gatekeepers, weeding out material that is not ready for the marketplace. They represent authors but also are friends of the publishing houses. Editors often initiate contact with agents who have brought them good manuscripts in the past, seeking to be given priority for upcoming projects.

As with anything, an agent's assessment of a manuscript's quality is subjective. Experienced agents typically gravitate toward certain areas of comfort and specialization, as do editors. If you can find an agency that specializes in your area of interest, you've got someone who knows where you're coming from.

Agents like to discover new talent. If you have something new and interesting to say and are able to say it well, they *want* to like your work. Agents need to sell manuscripts to publishers to stay in business. Unless an agent has one major client that requires most of his energy, agents are always open to the next new talent.

What Makes a Good Agent?

Anyone can call himself an agent, but a good literary agent will have had some prior connection with the publishing industry before hanging out his shingle. An agent's value is not just in ability to advocate your work but also in his access to publishers. After reading over your manuscript, he should have the names of several houses and editors to whom he wants to submit your book and be able to tell you why he thinks each publishing house would be a good potential fit for your work. He should demonstrate a fluent knowledge of the industry.

An agent does not work *for* the writer but rather on *behalf* of the writer. When you sign with an agent, you are giving him the power to act for or represent your interests. He will become your professional face when dealing with publishers. A good agent knows how to close a deal. While negotiating with both parties to create a meeting of the minds, he will act with your best interests in mind, working for the best monetary advance and terms possible.

As an author, you can, of course, submit your proposal directly to those publishing houses that accept unagented submissions, but even at those houses, an agent can give you more leverage. Individual authors can't have the kind of access that agents have to publishers no matter how savvy they are. A good agent should be able to pick up a phone and get through to an editor without having to plead with her assistant. If the agent has a good reputation for bringing in quality manuscripts and working ethically, his calls will be answered and his submissions will go right to the top of the editor's in-box.

Finding an Agent

As writers, we are highly vulnerable to anything that seems to bring us closer to our goal. Not all agents are equal, however, and you are cautioned to be leery of those who ask for "reader's fees" and of any other literary "service" that asks for money up front before agreeing to work with you. Reader's fees are charges to read, evaluate, and represent an author's submission. A few legitimate agents who specialize in representing novice authors do charge reading fees, since the likelihood of a sale and commission is somewhat less for first-time authors. Still, the practice of charging a reading fee is subject to abuse by unscrupulous agents. In my opinion, if an agency asks for a fee to read your work, it has found a very good source of income, but it is not necessarily interested in or capable of representing you.

Most reputable agents don't charge these fees; instead, they work on commission, usually 15 percent of the author's advance and royalties, meaning that the agent doesn't get paid until he places the manuscript with the publisher and the author gets paid. For such agencies, reading manuscripts is simply a cost of doing business, not a source of income. If you're unsure about the quality of your manuscript, you may be better off finding and paying for an outside editor, honing your work, and then trying to locate an agent who finds your work strong enough to represent without a reading fee.

To obtain names of agents, you can write the Association of Authors' Representatives (AAR) and ask for a list of their members (see "Spirit-Friendly Resources" for contact information). You can also visit your library to look at the current year's versions of *The Writer's Digest Guide to*

Literary Agents and the *Literary Market Place* (*LMP*). In these listings you will find some agents who are members of the AAR and others who are not. If an agent lists "all categories of nonfiction" as acceptable for submission, you can take a chance, but you are probably better off as a spiritual writer with an agent specifically interested in representing spiritual, occult, New Age, or religious material than if you sign with an agent who is more of a generalist.

Another good place to look for agents is in books that are similar to what you are writing. Often you'll find the agent's name on the acknowledgments page. If an author thanks his agent, you can be sure the agent did well for him.

One problem spiritual writers sometimes face in finding and keeping an agent is letting their sense of mission get in the way of following publishing protocols. As a spiritual writer, do not fall into the trap of thinking that your book is preordained to be published. Publishing, even of spiritual books, is a business first and foremost; those who know how to play the game will win. You can certainly be guided by intuition as to where to make your submissions, but this is where you use your know-how, savvy, logic, and brains. The spirit may guide you, but you need to take the lead.

Because agents are inundated with submissions, many improperly submitted proposals are summarily dismissed. So be sure to request their submission guidelines beforehand and then adhere to all of them. Some agents' policies are to automatically reject anything unsolicited, except for query letters, so submit your proposal and manuscript only when asked to do so. Your book may be the next greatest work of spiritual literature, but these agents will still not look at it if it has not been requested. It is possible that your manuscript will make it to "ye olde slush pile," but it is just as possible that it will become lost there, never to be seen again. Agents do not have an obligation to read something just because you have sent it to them.

If you are sending multiple submissions to several agents, which is a perfectly acceptable and expected practice, keep track of the names of the agents to whom you sent your queries and indicate in your query letter that it is a multiple submission. In chapter 12, we'll look at what happens if one of those submissions hits its mark and you get an offer of representation.

When you have an agent behind you, you feel a sense of validation, and spiritual agents are a special blessing. If you are fortunate to sign with one, you will find much more than an advocate. You will share a journey together. Selling books requires teamwork. The partnership between a spiritual agent and writer can be a powerful one. As a spiritual writer, remember that the agent knows what he or she is doing. Let go and let spirit work through both of you.

Now that we've looked at the people who will help you on your journey, let's look at the query letter and the proposal—the keys to opening the door to your publishing career.

10

THE QUERY LETTER

A query letter is a sales pitch to an agent or editor designed to interest him in your book idea. It has two purposes; first, to persuade him that the book will be profitable for him; and second, to showcase your writing skills. If you write a query that does not look like the dog chewed it, doesn't smell like stale cigarette smoke—yes, your paper will betray you!—and is not handwritten, it is very likely that an editor or agent will at least skim it. You want to make those seconds count.

Elements of the Query Letter

The query letter asks, "Here is my idea for a book; would you like to see more?" Because query letters should be only one page long, maximum two, choose your words carefully. It is your first introduction and your key to moving further in the process.

The Tone to Take

Be simple and to the point, but not so succinct that you entirely squash your personality. Finding your voice and balance for a good query letter is just like finding your writer's voice. You may need several drafts to get it right, but it will be well worth it. If you are unsure, opt for clarity over charm.

It is sometimes difficult for spiritual writers to avoid being overly passionate in query letters. Be yourself, but if you tend to be effusive, reign yourself in enough to fit on the page. Agents and editors see so many letters that they are not impressed with ecstasy or unsupportable claims. You will have as much success with hype as you will if you include a note from your mother saying what a special person you are.

No gimmicks. If the query does not have merit, no amount of chocolate, balloons, sing-o-grams, or expensive gifts will change that. The book industry is not Hollywood. Agents and editors do not want to be wowed. They want to be given something tangible to work with that they understand.

Write in a respectful, relatively formal, and clear manner. You can be friendly, but do not cross the line into unearned familiarity, even if you have met the agent or editor briefly. If you have met her at a conference, be sure to mention the meeting and include a detail that will help her recall your conversation from the scores of others she might have had. Do not assume that her polite interest in you at that time will elevate your submission over the others she receives. It is your call whether or not to use her first name in the salutation. Some don't like it and others don't care.

You may feel compelled to explain in your query a great deal about why you are writing, who you are, what your personal spiritual path is like, and other details that you feel may enhance the reader's connection to you. Those of us on a spiritual path seem to be attracted to kindred souls and want to make it a point to communicate that we are somehow all a part of the same club. Rest assured that a spiritually oriented agent or publisher—especially one who says it out loud and in print—is going to sense who you are and your connection to the divine. You speak the same language without saying a word. Just assume that there is no cosmic connection and stick to the facts at hand: your book and why it's a great opportunity for the reader of your letter.

The Letter's Contents

A good query letter answers specific, somewhat standardized questions, each of which is discussed briefly here and in more detail in chapter 11,

"The Book Proposal." Both the query letter and the proposal need to address these issues, although in the proposal you have more space to elaborate.

1. *What is the book about?* It is vital that the hook be made clear right from the start. There is nothing more frustrating for an agent or editor than to read an entire letter and ask, "What on earth is the book about?" Sometimes we read letters that have *something* compelling, but if we have to work too hard to figure out what it is, it is not worth our time.

Your first sentence is the most important one: Write a creative lead that tells the reader what your book is about and hooks him into wanting to learn more about your idea. And don't forget the number-one rule in writing: *Remember your audience.* Consider the reader's needs; make sure you are answering the implied question, "What's in this for me (or my literary agency, or my publishing house)?"

2. *Who is the market for the book?* Have a clear idea of a defined audience for your book. Is it single women under thirty, office workers seeking spirituality in the workplace, parents wanting to counteract the materialism in society? The one thing you should definitely not say is, "My book will appeal to anyone seeking a richer spiritual life," or some other vague statement. Be specific, and if possible, back up your intended audience with statistics from newspaper or magazine articles. For example, for a book on nurturing children's spirituality, you might say, "*Time* recently noted that 70 percent of parents feel that their child's spiritual training is not as complete as their own." This sort of statement establishes a need for your book and makes a publisher want to answer that need.

3. *How does the book differ from other similar books on the market?* Do some research using the on-line book retailers or your local bookstores or library to find out what books are already addressing your topic. Familiarize yourself with these books so you can clearly articulate how your book addresses the subject from a newer, fresher angle, without rehashing previously published material.

If there are no books on the market on your subject, that can either be great or not so great. It may either indicate a gaping hole that's crying to be filled by a quality book or a topic that nobody is interested in writing or reading about. Either way, don't ignore the competition. A publisher won't.

4. *Why are you the best person to write this book?* If you have credentials such as a degree or other education related to your book's topic, or a publishing history, include them. Keep your cited credentials relevant to your book so that it does not appear that you are insecure and overselling. This is a professional business letter and not an exercise in approval seeking. Do not allow a tone of neediness in your letter, or you will raise a red flag of being potentially "high maintenance."

5. *How will you help promote the book?* Show your publishing savvy by indicating that you as an author are prepared to help market and promote your book. See the "Marketing and Publicity" section in chapter 11 for specifics.

Query Letter Taboos

Your query letter will have a much greater chance of being taken seriously if you avoid the following statements:

- *Ten other agents/publishers rejected my manuscript but I know you will have the intelligence to see its value.* An appeal to the reader's vanity will not overcome his sense of foreboding when he reads this.
- *My book will be a best-seller.* Maybe, but it's really not up to you to say.
- *Oprah or Sally will love this book.* Oh yeah? Everyone says this.
- *I am the next James Redfield/Brian Weiss/Marianne Williamson/John Gray, etc.* Puh-leeze.
- *My manuscript has been read and endorsed by Famous Author X.* Some famous authors will give a favorable book quote to anyone who

asks them. Agents and publishers know who these people are—
and so will you if you peruse enough book jackets—and their
names mean little.

- *Dear Sir or Madam.* If a writer doesn't have enough initiative to find
  out an agent's or editor's name and title, then they can be sure the
  author probably doesn't have enough initiative to be a professional writer. I've never yet met an editor or agent named Sir or
  Madam. (The one exception is those places that request you
  address submissions to Acquisitions Editor, or some such. In this
  case, it would be appropriate.)
- *I got your name from Person X.* Usually, a referral doesn't make much
  of a difference. Some publishing houses will, as a courtesy, read
  anything that comes through one of their published authors.
- *God told me to write to you.* This sort of statement is a red flag, even
  if it is true. To the uninitiated, it can cause you to appear strange.
  To those on the path, it will indicate a spiritual immaturity.

Here are some more *don'ts*:

- *Don't forget to proofread your own letter for typos or grammatical errors.* Agents
  and publishers love words! Avoidable errors raise their hackles.
- *Don't pack your letter so densely with type that it's difficult to read.* Editors
  and agents read all day, and their eyes get tired. Include plenty of
  white space and visual breaks like subheads to open your letter up
  and keep their eyes from crossing.
- *Don't brag.* You are writing to inform and to offer a mutually beneficial proposition, not to impress someone with how wonderful
  you are.
- *Don't forget to include your SASE (self-addressed, stamped envelope).*
- *Don't handwrite your letter.* Surprisingly, this still happens. Instant
  reject.

- *Don't fax queries, call to pitch an idea, or ask for a meeting.* This is a breach of protocol. No matter how good you can make something sound on the telephone, you will invariably hear either, "I have to see it first; send a query," or "We don't accept phone queries." Such encounters are discouraging and can also bias the editor or agent against you, making them remember you for the wrong reason.

- *Don't query by e-mail before finding if that's acceptable.* Most publishers will not accept e-mail submissions. Publishers create elaborate systems to keep track of the enormous amount of submissions they receive. E-mails don't fit into these systems very well and can be hard to read. Please follow the publisher's guidelines to the letter. You are not an exception to the rule.

- *After sending your query, don't call, e-mail, or write to ask, "Did you receive it?" or "Did you read it yet?"* If you get no answer in what you think is an unreasonably long time (give them at least a month), mail another letter. It is possible that the first one got lost. It happens—all the time. Do not reprimand the agent or editor for not getting back at you. Remember, there is no obligation on anyone's part to even read your letter. Most agents and editors are kind; they will try to get back to people within a reasonable time, so don't fret too much. Meditate, pray, or write in your journal.

- *Don't insist the reader must read your entire manuscript because there's no other way to truly grasp the importance/beauty/truth of the message.* The message of your manuscript is only one of several things that agents and publishers learn from your query. They also learn how professional you are—an indication of what you would be like to work with—and whether you understand your own writing well enough to convey the book's essence in the way you would need to as a published author. Don't bother begging them to read the whole thing. We assure you, they won't.

Examples of Query Letters

Strong

The letter below, written by a first-time author, was enticing enough that the publishers of this book requested to see his full proposal. The book was signed up, and the rest is history.

There is no formula for a successful query, however. Don't feel bound by the structure or compelled to follow this one as a model—but do note the clarity and conciseness.

Cynthia Black
Editor in Chief

Dear Ms. Black,

As a writer and photographer, I am looking to develop a long-term relationship with a full-service trade publisher specializing in creativity, spirituality, and personal growth. Your name has been mentioned repeatedly as an editor/publisher that may have interest in my work.

I am seeking to place a recently completed book on creativity and awareness that, despite some initial inquiries, has not yet been marketed to publishers. For the sake of my own clarity and focus, I've needed to nurture the unfoldment of the entire spectrum of ideas before going public. The book, however, has been tested extensively in the college classroom, on the lecture circuit, and in adult workshop programs with great success.

Enclosed is an expanded table of contents for *The Widening Stream: A Guide to the Seven Stages of the Creative Process*, along with a short biography. If you are interested, I can supply the completed manuscript or sample chapters. I have outlined an entire series on creativity and visual perception and would be happy to send you the table of contents for other possible books as well.

The book was written with two target audiences in mind: the mainstream mind/body/spirit market and the college/university classroom. Between overly complex works written by psychologists or philosophers and limited, idealistic, over-simplified treatments of the theme lie a broad region of need. For example, there is not a single general book on creativity that is widely used in college classes in art, creative writing, or new media studies. Nor am I aware of a single book, designed for the general reader, on learning to see and cultivating the deeper potentials of human perception. I hope to help fill these gaps.

Sincerely,
David Ulrich

This letter is strong because it is

- Brief
- To the point
- Professional
- Conscious of how the material fits the house profile

Weak

The letter below is an amalgam of the types of letters regularly received by editors and agents, the kind that causes them to heave sighs of exhaustion:

Dear Acquistions Editor,

After asking for Guidance to help me communicate the Truth, i.e., spiritual concepts and practices, I found my way to you. Right now we live at one of the most crucial junctures in the history of mankind. Experts have reported that in the next twenty-five years, humanity will decide key factors that will affect the earth's environment and culture for the next hundred thousand years.

And yet we are surrounded on all sides with turmoil and confusion. While polls are showing that people continue to feel general satisfaction with their lives, evidence is everywhere that our traditional institutions and dearest values are crumbling.

For those that are skeptical about the world's fate ignore the lessons of history. These individuals tend to cherish past memories of the old days when things were better, and passively await the decline of society.

The good news can be clearly seen if we look closely at human history: A new vision of hope can arise out of the chaos and crises, like the phoenix rising out of the ashes. And this is the new hope I want to give the world, a book that I call *Holy Rising*. The goal is to cultivate the tiny seeds of kindness and love that are buried within each of us, bringing light to a new world that is already emerging.

Inspirational books have started topping best-seller lists, proving that in the midst of the turmoil and confusion that is disrupting people's lives, they are seeking some sort of guidance. In fact, Gallup polls have shown that individuals who want personal ispiration [sic] and growth soared from 18 percent in 1983 to 82 percent in 1999!

While books about humanity's evolution and a new vision of the future exist, they tend to be written for those who already have a more liberal and optimistic view of mankind's chances of improving. My book, on the other hand, is geared specifically toward the larger population, the ones who are cynical and dubious about the future. These individuals need a new perspective of the way human evolution and current events intertwine, with lots of clear, grounded information. Unlike most inspirational books out there, mine is rooted in specific examples and extensive research, plus many examples.

There are two parts to *Holy Rising*. The first part goes to the reader's heart. Validating everything they feel about the world. As a diamond is polished to expose its lovely surface beneath, I point out that the troubles in the world are actually an important part of the process of transformation that is now occurring. To convince a skeptical reader, I ground my claims in the work of famous theorists such as Freud and Marx. After a thorough synthesis of their work, I propose that there are several identifiable characteristics in our evolution. But to learn what these are, you will need to request our manuscript.

In the second section I carefully review how these processes can be seen in every part of society, from government to health, from education to personal growth. It also gives the reader some tools to personally become a catalyst for this new vision. There has never been such an important time to publish a book that answers this need. It is time for world transformation, and *Holy Rising* is sure to lead the way.

When you respond, please let me know your marketing plans for the book, as well as any suggestions for agents that you may have.

Many thanks,
Wanna B. Righter

The most obvious flaws of this letter are that the writer

- Begins with an irrelevant opening statement
- Rambles and takes too long to get to the point

- Is repetitive
- Makes vague, undemonstrable generalizations and empty promises
- Didn't bother to research the correct recipient
- Makes demands of the publisher
- Didn't check for typos

The Importance of the Query Letter

Compared with the task of writing an entire book, query letters are not difficult. You have already worked hard to bring yourself to the point where it is appropriate to send one, so be sure to make the query a reflection of the work you have already done.

Every part of the process toward publication is important. Inspiration is a gift, but knowing how to get published is a skill. Each step in the process forms a foundation for the next. Put your spirit into this letter as much as you have the rest of your book, but keep it within the parameters of professional business correspondence. Remember to relax, allow your inner voice to write, and then employ your inner editor.

If you skip the query letter and send an unsolicited proposal or manuscript to a publisher, you may never hear anything back. If you include an SASE with enough postage—which you should always, always do—you will hear back from the publisher. Eventually. If they send back your manuscript with a rejection letter, don't be surprised if your manuscript appears completely untouched. It is nothing personal. Editors and agents will sometimes pick through and skim the slush pile looking for gems, but most do not have the time. It is acceptable to send several query letters simultaneously. Just indicate in each that you are sending multiple submissions.

And finally, before you send off your query letter, make sure you have a proposal or manuscript ready. There is nothing more annoying to an agent or editor than getting excited about a book that doesn't even exist.

When you write and send out any kind of submission, just say a prayer that your letter or proposal arrives where it needs to arrive. Other than that, you pretty much have to let it go. Everything happens as it is supposed to, but we don't always know what the "supposed to" is. Remember that sometimes our writing is for the purpose of growing our souls. Sometimes no matter how hard we try, the universe has a different plan for us.

11

THE BOOK PROPOSAL

Publishers can't publish every book that interests them. While many publishers of spiritual material have a mission to publish books to benefit humankind, the bottom line for them is simple: Can we make money on it so we can stay in business? It's your job to show them why your book is not only interesting but has a demonstrable market and is financially viable. Your book proposal is, therefore, essentially a sales document to persuade a busy agent or editor either to represent you or to publish your book. It anticipates their questions and provides answers and support to your claim that your book is worthy of being published.

Agents and publishers are always swamped. Always. They don't have time to read every manuscript. They want you to condense your message and make it easy for them to figure out if they want to do business with you. A great proposal provides everything an agent or editor needs to make a decision. If done correctly, it will make them happy because you've made their job easier. They will like you even before they meet you, and we all know that we prefer to do business with people we like.

Even after your proposal has sold an editor on the merits of your idea, it does not get set aside. It is used to sell your book to people all along the publishing pipeline. First, editors pitch your book to their editorial review committee, where a good proposal gives the editor persuasion at her fingertips. She will be asked questions about the book's sales potential, and if you write an effective proposal, she can answer any question without hesitation. She'll be confident about your book, and that confidence will be contagious.

Once the book gets past a publisher's own editorial review committee, it has to be "sold" to the publisher's distributor or to their own marketing department or sales force to convince them that your book will be a moneymaker. Once that happens, the sales team will in turn pitch your book to their national sales reps, who will then use the information from your proposal to be an advocate for your book when they present it to bookstore owners and buyers for the large chains. These store owners decide, after a brief one-minute presentation about your book, how many copies to order. So you see that, at every step, the information in your proposal can be used to generate buzz and interest (*code*: sales) in your book.

When it comes to selling your book, don't leave it up to faith and good intentions. Master the craft of the book proposal.

What Comes First—the Proposal or the Manuscript?

Many nonfiction books are sold from a proposal even if the manuscript has been completed. But you might find yourself with an advance before you even finish the book, if every element in your proposal is good enough and the agent or editor has confidence in your ability to carry out what you have promised—in other words, if you show writing ability and experience in meeting deadlines. This is unlikely for first-time authors but not unheard of.

If you write and submit the proposal before you have written an entire manuscript, you won't waste time on projects that are time-sensitive or that have no market. If your proposal is rejected, the rejection might help you determine that your book's topic may need to be altered in some way.

Another advantage of selling your idea by proposal is possibly getting the input of the publishing house while you are writing the book. An editor may have a vision for the book that enhances its scope, substance, or marketability. If you haven't written the complete book, this vision can be incorporated at an early developmental stage, and you can avoid extensive revisions. The final result will be a higher-quality, more saleable book.

If you sell your idea this way, you might also have the advantage of gaining the input of other members of the publishing house, such as its marketing and publicity staff. As a writer hoping to be published, you are only one player; you can't possibly know all of the nuances of book marketing and distribution. It's hard sometimes to let go of the purity of your message, but if you can develop trust in your agent or publisher—or both—to hone your book (*code*: edit your book) so that it meets its broadest audience, you'll have forged a solid team, all with the goal of bringing the best book possible to the greatest number of readers.

Writing the Proposal

You know that your hook is your most important ammunition. So begin there and build your proposal around it. Statistics or concrete statements will help you, but since that is not always possible for spiritual books, try to keep your credibility and promotability, the existence of a market for your book, and the quality of your message front and center. While you shouldn't assume that the person reading the proposal speaks your same spiritual language, publishers and agents are recognizing the appeal of these books more and more. Write your proposal for the uninitiated. Your purpose is to find a publisher, not to convert her.

Do not include too much hype or fluff before getting to the meat of the book, or that may be all anyone sees. Make your writing tight and effective and be sure it clearly states your hook. Every section of your proposal is important, so use the same energy on each; you never know how much weight your prospective publisher gives certain information.

Everyone has their own interests in evaluating a project. Do not skip any sections or you will be wasting an opportunity to persuade.

You want to be in control of the information; you don't want the reader drawing the wrong conclusions because, despite your awesome message, your proposal is incomplete. And then there's the human factor—if the agent or editor is having a bad day, you are out of luck. An incomplete or amateurish proposal will merit a growl or a moan and a toss into the reject pile.

Proposal lengths vary. Some are short, some might as well be manuscripts. But longer is not always better, especially in the word business. Don't repeat yourself, oversell with hyperbole, or ramble. Find your balance, use your inner voice, and make your proposal whatever length you feel will adequately address the points we'll cover below.

After you write your proposal, set it aside. Read it a week or two later when you can be objective. Then pretend you are an agent or editor. What questions might they have as they read? We have evaluated proposals where the only thing running through our mind was, What credentials does the author have to write such a book? Obviously, the author did not address this question. Make sure you do not make the same mistake.

While there is room for creativity, stick fairly closely to the following format so you can be sure you have not left out anything needed to present your book. Let's look at the standard proposal elements:

Title and Subtitle

Run these by a few objective friends. While publishers often change a book's title during the editing process, a bad one can be a turnoff, especially at the proposal stage when every word counts. A title is a key marketing tool. Don't make it confusing or depressing. Even if your book is on grief, choose a title that emphasizes hope or help, not despair. Avoid clichés.

Don't pick a title that is so obscure that its meaning becomes clear only after extensive explanation. You will not be sitting next to the editor when she reads your proposal to explain to her what your title really means. If it needs explaining, it's not a good title. A title should tell and sell. If you do choose a title that offers no insight into the book's contents but is still strong, then make sure your subtitle gives the reader an idea of what your book will cover. Study titles and subtitles at a bookstore. They are important.

Overview

The overview sets the tone. If the overview is strong, it increases the reader's desire to find something more that is likable and saleable in the rest of the proposal. For a reader this is a much different vantage point than having a bias against something and looking for reasons to reject it.

Your overview should begin like a query letter, with a clear statement of your book's name, thesis, and hook. It should briefly address what the book is about, why it should exist, who will buy it, and why you are the best person to write it. It can even include a few of your very best—*short*—excerpts from the book. Do not be grandiose or vague. After you set a concise professional tone in the overview, later in the proposal you can be more dramatic and creative.

Do *not* say, "I've been intrigued by and read a lot about subject x for years and have some free time now that my children are grown and have decided to share my discoveries." Amateurish. No matter what you say after that bit of personal revelation, you are climbing uphill.

The overview is your first opportunity to persuade, to show you are a professional writer, so make it count.

Congruency with the Publisher's List

Show that you've done your homework. Look up the Web site of each publisher to whom you will send your proposal. What is the overall tone, topics, and market they cover with their books? Your book should fit in with their list. If you can find titles that it complements, so much the better. For example, let them know that your book would be a perfect complementary title to their recent release, *Book X*, or would fit wonderfully in their series on women who take a different path. Make the editor feel that your book belongs at their house, and support your statements with details.

Markets and Audience

Who will buy your book? If you know your market, you will know if you have a viable book. The more specific you are, the more your proposal's recipient will have confidence that you understand the connection between books and business.

Determining your market is not as difficult as it sounds. As you are considering all the possibilities, you may discover that you have affiliations that would represent a segment of your market. For example, people who attend seminars on your topic are your market. Know which magazines might carry an article on your subject. Its readers are your audience. Find out the circulation number of such magazines by looking in the annual *Writer's Market*. Anything that can create a sense of numbers will add to your credibility and weigh in your favor.

This is again where knowing your genre is so important. When you know specifically where your book would be shelved at a bookstore, you are more credible when you explain who the market is for your book. It is common for writers to indicate a market so broad that it has no real meaning to anyone. There are many permutations of spirituality. Know which audience is yours. A born-again Christian is interested in spiritual growth. So is a Wiccan. Are they buying the same books? No.

Another market to consider is the foreign market. Does your book have potential to be sold overseas, or to "travel"? If yes, that's a big plus for you because the publisher could sell the foreign rights to your book as a secondary source of publishing income. At this moment, certain topics such as intuition, animal communication, and personal growth are big overseas, though they could become dated at any moment. To learn more about what sorts of titles other countries are publishing, attend book fairs like the annual Book Expo America in the United States and the London Book Fair or the Frankfurt Book Fair. If you lack the budget to travel, *Publishers Weekly* issues a book-fair report on foreign-rights sales. See "Spirit-Friendly Resources" for more places to research topics that appeal to foreign bookbuyers.

As you write your book proposal, do not confuse markets and audience with marketing and publicity. In your section on publicity, you'll describe ways you will help your publisher to sell your book and strategies and contacts you can bring to the plan.

Competition

This is where you face the other books like yours head on. Before writing any book, be aware of what has already been published on the topic. If you have a topic similar to someone else's, this just means you need to justify how yours presents a fresh perspective or how you are uniquely qualified based on your credentials.

This is the hard-core business section of your proposal. The person reading it is going to look at what you present and translate it into the number of books that can be sold. Don't forget the costs involved in producing a book. If the market is already too full it will not pay for the publisher to add another book to the feeding frenzy. You want them to see that your book could be part of a new trend, will fill a niche not yet crowded with other books, or has a unique angle that differentiates it from other books on the topic. Of course this needs to be the truth. If it isn't, find another book to write.

Certain subjects can sustain only a few books in the marketplace. Other subjects can always welcome new and fresh perspectives. And take heart—booksellers are in the business of selling *new* books. They need to have fresh takes, even on old subjects. There are only so many topics under the sun, yet millions of books are sold each year. If you can say something in a fresh way, even on a familiar subject, you've got a marketable book— as long as you can get people to understand what makes yours stand out.

Check out bookstores, on-line booksellers such as Bodhitree.com, book clubs, and catalogs such as One Spirit to see current books coming out in the spiritual market. Become an expert on what is out there so you can be persuasive on why your book will be filling a need that has yet to be met. Show how other similar books actually establish a market for the one you are proposing.

Think of the competition in terms of how it actually benefits you. It is never effective to say that there is no competition, even if you believe this to be true. If there is truly no competition or anything remotely like your book, there may be a good reason. Maybe no one wants a book like yours. Lastly, avoid trashing other books. This does not reflect well on you and will come back to haunt you.

Marketing and Publicity

Writing a book is one piece of the publishing puzzle. Another hugely important piece is your experience and willingness to publicize your work; it can be the deciding factor in a publisher's selecting your book for publication. Editors look for writers who are savvy about the business side of publishing. Your input is valuable, especially if you are an expert on your topic. If you're a first-time author, the publisher needs to establish your credibility with book buyers and to book you as a guest on radio or television shows. It is challenging for publishers to promote an unknown author, but you can help by working to enhance your credibility, as we discussed in part one.

Following are some possible ways to highlight your ability to market your book. Not all will apply to you, of course, but the point is that as an author, you are expected to actively participate in publicity.

- Speaking at seminars connected to your book's subject, or holding your own
- Teaching classes on your topic, either in person or on-line
- Having radio or television savvy for interviews about your book
- Being a recognized expert in your field, one whom the media may call on for quotes or analysis on your book's subject
- Getting connected to influential (sales-enhancing) people who could provide a quote or foreword for your book
- Making yourself available for bookstore readings and signings in the first few months after your book is published
- Being able to hire your own publicist or purchase a certain number of your own books
- Writing magazine articles to stimulate interest in your book
- Being a member of an organization that could offer opportunities for you to speak and promote your book
- Having a viable connection to any facet of the media
- Traveling overseas, if your book has international potential

If you have the time to travel, your willingness to promote your book in the United States and abroad is a plus. Remember, people speak English all over the globe. Universities, associations, and bookstores in Europe like to invite English-speaking authors for events.

The ideas for promotion are endless. In some situations you will have support from your publisher, who will set up some initial publicity for you. However, in your book proposal create a plan that does not assume anything about what the publisher might do. In fact, do not refer to the publisher at all. And don't tell them you are waiting to hear what they can do for you.

Do not say things like, "This is just the kind of book Montel and Oprah like." Practically every proposal these days claims this. Unless you have a personal relationship with these shows, this is a throwaway. You may find a good publicist or can build yourself to the point where you can make it on your own, but do not rely on miracles. Book proposals need facts or at least tangible possibilities.

If you have few hard leads to offer in this section, at least show that you're willing to do whatever it takes to promote your book. You can contact organizations or bookstores to see what it would take to set up book signings. Be creative. Moxie costs less than spending money. The more practical your book is, the more forums there are through which you can sell it. This is what agents and editors want to see. Your ability and willingness to market your book can elevate your project above the others in an editor's in-box.

Author's Qualifications

Even when a publisher or agent finds your proposal compelling, she will immediately look at your credentials to determine if you are the right person to write the book. This may seem silly since you are the one presenting the idea. But the author is part of the package. Many good book ideas have been rejected because the author was not seen as being a marketable-enough presence for the book's contents.

Your job will be to anticipate this issue so they can be convinced that both you and the book are right for them. But you can't make stuff up. If you can't do it on your own, then maybe you need to look for another book or seek a collaborator who has the credentials you lack. This happens all the time. People with doctorates collaborate with authors who are looking to build their own reputations. You may share the billing on the cover, but you get your book on the shelf, and that's the name of the game, isn't it?

Any exceptional experiences like spending ten years in a monastery, having a Ph.D. in the field, or studying in Tibet would be impressive. If you have not done any of these things, however, do not be intimidated.

These experiences, while interesting, do not make one person more spiritual than another.

If your credentials and background are not relevant to the book, be creative. But don't ramble and include things that are extraneous or stretch so far you seem plain silly. If experience isn't your strong suit, then make up for it everywhere else in the proposal with stellar writing.

Media experience can be repeated here. Any publishing history is good and any relevant awards can be included too. Again, a personal touch is OK, but do not be too cute. Your biography is a window into the person behind the words. As in everything you do, find your own balance. Make sure your bio feels like you.

In addition to your book idea, agents and publishers are also evaluating the risk of working with a new author. Show that you are a good risk for carrying out your contract. Keep every agreement you make, even if it's just to return a phone call or e-mail the editor with some specific piece of information she has requested. Some people are wonderful at persuasion but not at follow-through. Publishers know that; they've been burned, so in your proposal, establish your credibility as a person who has met deadlines and who can deliver a professional product.

Table of Contents

As we discussed in chapter 6, the table of contents is the backbone of your book. It will serve as a blueprint for you when you write the book, and it will give your agent or editor a quick view of where the book is heading. It is an indication of your logic and how well you have developed the potential of your book. In fact, some agents and editors skip right from your overview to the table of contents. Do not skimp here, because it is yet another opportunity to influence their decision.

For the proposal, include each chapter's subheads in your table of contents. Chapter titles alone are sometimes not too informative, so including subheads gives the reader, should she want it, more detail about the book. Another effective technique, one that requires strong writing skills, is to include the first sentence in each chapter after the chapter title in the table of contents. If the first line is strong and compelling, the editor will want to flip right away to that chapter to read "the rest of the story."

Chapter Outline

Another way to provide a quick overview of your book's contents is to include a chapter-by-chapter outline—a paragraph or two summarizing the contents of each chapter. Think of each chapter as a magazine article, with a beginning, middle, and end. Use your most compelling writing in this synthesis; it may be all an editor has time to read. Don't include too much detail in each summary.

Selected Chapters

If you are an unpublished writer or are writing about an unusual subject, it is imperative that the publisher receive sample material. One to three chapters is standard. Many editors prefer that you send chapters in order, but that is your call. In nonfiction, chapters are typically self-contained, so you could select chapters at random.

These chapters should be better than anything you have ever written. This is really important. Even if everything in your proposal up to this point has been strong, if you're not able to deliver strong, supported, clear, organized, and thought-provoking writing in your actual book, that'll be the end of the line for you. Publishers see many great ideas in proposals, ideas that they get excited about. They are often disappointed, however, because in the execution of the idea, authors fail to deliver on their promise.

It takes practice, but it is important for your proposal to show consistent quality and effort from beginning to end. Don't assume that because you know what you have to say, the agent or editor will have enough insight to take your word for it. Always have someone with a cold eye read your chapters and point out where you need to clarify, organize, or tighten before you send your work out into the world.

Tone

Never say, in your proposal, "God told me to write this" or "My psychic told me it would be a best-seller." This may be true. You may also have had a vision of the Blessed Virgin. But keep this to yourself. This kind of fervor will raise a red flag even with spirit-friendly agents and publishers. Wide-eyed naïveté and unchanneled enthusiasm can be charming—but not when it comes to selling your book. Even if your subject matter is esoteric or channeled, highly interpretative or intuitive, your book proposal needs to be rooted in the realities of the publishing business.

Faith and connection to your inner voice will give you the creativity and inspiration to write, but do not count on people understanding your inner language. Agents and editors do not have to be "on the path" to be effective. Be clear in your communication. Stay grounded.

Presentation

You do not have to spend a fortune on fancy binders and expensive paper for your proposal. Just make sure everything is neat and professionally presented. Leave your proposal unbound, because if it generates interest, agents and editors will make copies of it.

Do not package your proposal so that no one can open it without a crowbar or a bomb. It's unlikely that anything will happen to it in the mail. And as with query letters, do not use gimmicks. One agent once received a proposal that had somehow been infused with dryer sheets to make it smell good, and she almost passed out with an allergic reaction. If you smoke, have a copy made somewhere where it will smell fresh, and do not annoint your paper with essential oils or perfumes either.

Never send originals of artwork, photographs, or your manuscript. If you are sending a one-of-a-kind original or your only copy, you are setting yourself up for unhappiness. A publisher or agent has no obligation to carefully guard your originals. Things get misplaced when you are dealing with hundreds of pieces of paper each day. Some publishers and agencies are remarkably organized. But you can't count on that. We don't know of any firm that as yet lists "organized" as one of its credentials.

How Can I Avoid Rejection?

Stay under the covers! Rejection is a part of life and an inevitable part of the writing journey. The only way to avoid rejection is to not submit your work anywhere. Even if your proposal and book are perfectly executed, they will not be for everybody. There could be a million reasons why your proposal was rejected, none of which reflect on you as a person. Selling any product is simply a matter of numbers—you have to get it out there to as many likely prospects as possible before you get any nibbles. Any salesperson will tell you this. For instance, in direct-mail marketing campaigns, even those targeted to likely buyers of a product, a 2 percent response rate is considered success.

Rejection letters are a good thing. They give feedback. If you get enough of them, you may want to reevaluate your submission. You can also learn from a kind editor's specific comments as to why your book won't work for them. You don't have to contact that person again, so you can take her advice in the privacy of your own ego.

Every time you put your work out into the universe, you receive something that will help you achieve your destiny. Ask and you will receive. If you are putting your manuscript out there, you are essentially asking the universe, "Should this book exist? Who will benefit most from it?" You will get an answer one way or another.

Creating a successful proposal that generates interest is like putting together the pieces of a puzzle—the more pieces you put into place with strong writing and content, the more checks go into the mental "plus" column in the editor's head as she reads it. Enough checks and you'll be getting a phone call!

Sometimes strange things happen to bring manuscripts to the right people at the right time. So maintain your faith, your dignity, and your tenacity, because you never know when it will be the right time for you or when the right people will converge.

12

THE ROAD TO PUBLICATION

So you've created a proposal and manuscript in which every element shines. Let's look at what happens when an agent or publisher expresses interest in your manuscript and discuss how you can continue to build, during the courtship stage, the professional aura and attitude that will make you look like a sure bet as a publishing professional.

The Phone Interview

You've gotten a phone call; the publisher is interested. Hurray! They want to set up a phone conference with you to discuss your book. You're not at the point of getting an offer, so what's this all about? Well, as you now know, your book is just a part of the total marketing package; you are the other key component. Publishers may want to know how well you can speak extemporaneously and how enthusiastically you can describe yourself and your book. In short, they want to see if *you* are marketable. They might need you to do book-signings, radio and television interviews, and perhaps even seminars to generate interest in your book. If you're unable to speak off the cuff and with vigor, you may yet lose the sale.

Don't come off as blasé. When a publisher calls you to discuss your book, they have an agenda—maybe they want to hear how you sound, how enthusiastic you are, and how amenable you are to their suggestions for the book. Believe it or not, one prospective author, when asked about her topic in an initial phone call, answered, "Oh, I don't know, it's just something I've sort of been kicking around for a while. I'd actually forgotten about it—I've been working on this other thing." Maybe it was just natural reticence, but her lack of passion about her own book was a major red flag for the editor.

If you are a quiet or shy person, don't reply to the publisher's or editor's comments with monsyllables like "OK," "uh-huh," and "right." He wants to hear multiparagraphed, enthusiastic answers to questions. Now is not the time to be overly diffident, hesitant, or modest. He is looking for a self-promoter. Try to have some fresh information that further illustrates your book's contents. A publisher will see this as great fodder for radio interviews to publicize your book—the author who has a million stories or ideas and whose interview is not just a one-note rehash of the contents of her book. Be open to suggestions for your book's direction. Unless you want to publish it yourself, you need to show interest and enthusiasm for a publisher's vision for making your book more marketable.

On the other hand, if you are a gregarious person by nature and tend to talk too much, try to focus your enthusiasm. Don't repeat or overstate when the person on the other end has already gotten your point and may be starting to get restless. You aren't going to have trouble convincing him that you are outgoing enough to appear publicly, but he will then want to know that you can be coherent and interesting. And remember, stop selling when the sale is made. Overselling yourself might lose you the deal as well.

To prepare for this conversation, tape-record your voice and critique yourself; work to eliminate any "ums," "yeahs," and halting delivery. How's the tone of your voice? If it's quavery or nasal or whiny, do what you can toward a more mellifluous delivery. It seems ironic for an author to worry about his speaking voice, but that's the reality of being an author—your speaker's voice can be just as important as your writer's voice.

What Do I Do If I Am Given an Offer of Representation by an Agent?

When an agent requests an exclusive look at your manuscript, this means she wants the first opportunity to see the material in greater detail before any other agents have a chance to snap it up. And this means your query did the job of convincing her that you might have more there. Expressing interest for a first glance is only one step in the process, however. Don't put a deposit on a new car yet.

You are not obligated to offer an exclusive to anyone just because she asks any more than you are obligated to marry someone who likes you. If someone else is your first choice, ask if that agent has any interest. Sometimes telling an agent that another agent is requesting an exclusive can create just the right amount of competition between professionals that you need. (Be warned, however, that fabricating interest can lose you the deal—most agents can spot it a mile away.)

If you decide to agree to an exclusive, you should offer a short but reasonable period of time. If the agent is really interested, you should hear fairly quickly—from a few weeks to a month. You should follow up after the allotted time to determine if there is real interest and to see if you can reel in an offer. Sometimes the lack of response is a matter of time constraint and is not a reflection of an agent's interest in you. Unless you are a known quantity, your project may not be an immediate priority. If you have a tendency to obsess and worry, try not to wallow in thoughts of rejection until you have received them. Assume the best and politely check on the status of your submission. Do not nag; just inquire and make the agent aware of the expiration of the exclusive.

If the agent who requests the exclusive is your first choice, there will be an underlying expectation that if representation is offered, you will accept. There is little variation from the standard 15 percent commission, and at this stage, we don't recommend you shop further even if you are still getting responses. If you receive other requests for material, you can use this information to leverage a more expedient offer from your first-choice agent, but we do not recommend sending out manuscripts after receiving an offer that you are comfortable with.

If the first agent to respond is not your first choice, or if you receive several responses, it is best not to offer an exclusive even if one is requested. Be up front and indicate that it is a multiple submission but that you will keep the agent apprised. Make sure you are diligent about contacting any agents who have requested to review your manuscript should you decide to sign on with someone else. Agents do not earn anything unless they sell books, and it is not nice to waste people's time. If you are trying to hedge your bets by going behind people's backs, you may wind up with nothing.

Authors do not realize that although many books are published each year, there is a limited number of active agents. Eventually most good agents cross paths or at least hear about one another. There are also only so many editors. We had one client who had signed with us to represent one of her books. Unbeknownst to anyone but her, she signed a separate project with another agent. There is nothing illegal about this, as most contracts do not tie up authors for all of their books, but there was something she overlooked that cost her representation.

As we were shopping her book to publishers, the other agent was also shopping another of her books to the same publishers. The other agent was even more aghast than we were and dropped her immediately. We are not thrilled with client subterfuge, so we dropped the project we were representing. Eventually she realized it was her own fault and requested that we represent her again. We are softies, and we like her, so we did take her back. We have since developed a wonderful relationship. But you may not be so lucky. Writing is a business, but never underestimate the human factor.

When you receive an offer for book representation, you can shift the focus a bit from selling yourself to allowing the agent to do a bit of selling. There are varying opinions about this, but it is best not to put the agent on the hot seat—remember, you haven't made him any money yet. Unless you are already an established author, there is an expectation on the part of the agent that there will be a learning curve. The agent will be factoring in how well he can work with you and guide you toward both a sale and a successful career. Even though you have an offer, you are not completely in the driver's seat. For every accepted author there are many others vying for the same spot.

If you have done some of the preliminary research described in chapter 9, you will already know some things about the agency you have targeted, but you may want to know more. While you are justified in wanting clear information about the agency that will be helping you shape your future, it's important to hone your questions so they do not put the agent on the defensive. The last thing you want to do is cause him to question his decision to make the offer.

Some questions you can ask include

- How long have you been an agent?
- How many titles have you sold?
- May I see your list of client books sold to publishers?
- What is your commission rate?
- How and when am I to be paid?
- Do you require a contract, and what is the term?
- Can your contract be terminated at any time?
- Do you have anyone who handles film, television, audio, foreign, or other rights stemming from a publishing contract?
- Do you charge any expenses?

- How will you communicate with me regarding the status of my project?
- Where do I sign?

Most agents have a packet of material available that will answer most of your questions. We do not recommend that you ask overly technical questions in the context of making your decision. The matter at hand is to determine if there is a good match and for you to learn about how things will work for you directly.

When you are offered and accept representation, it is important for you to avoid trying to micromanage things. Most agents will keep you informed about changes in status, but they may not contact you immediately with every rejection. There are a certain number of rejections anticipated with a multiple submission to publishers, and the agent may choose to wait to go over them with you all at once to establish additional strategy for selling your book. This also prevents the dreaded writer-insecurity backlash. There is nothing worse for an agent trying to sell a book than a hysterical writer. We had one client who become so enraged about the rejections she was receiving that she went behind our backs directly to the publishers demanding an explanation. Needless to say, the result was embarrassing and not fruitful for anyone.

Agents assume a certain amount of risk in choosing to represent a project with a writer attached to it. Writers have the advantage of being able to fully research an agency, while agents often have to accept the writer's word. It becomes like the security questions you are asked at the airport: "Has anyone unknown to you given you any packages?" and "Have your bags been in your possession the entire time?" If you were doing something you are not supposed to do such as carrying contraband or leaving your bags unattended, would you tell someone? Similarly, agents can't ask you, "Are you insane, mentally unbalanced, and liable to drive us crazy with your constant unreasonable demands?" Is anyone going to say yes?

So if you are close to the edge and unwilling to admit it, at least consider that carefully building a relationship with your agent can be very beneficial to your overall writing career. A good agent is well-connected and can help you throughout the entire publishing process, far beyond just contract negotiation. Agents can not only advocate on your behalf, they can also find work for you. Agents often find projects that need good writers. Fiction writers can also benefit from a relationship with an agent that extends beyond the specific book offered for representation. Many novelists write nonfiction as a way to maintain a steady writing career. Fiction writers also find creative fulfillment in writing narrative nonfiction and may find opportunities through their agent that they might otherwise not find on their own.

Agents are not entirely unavailable to their clients during the process of the sale of a book. If you do not abuse the communication, your agent will keep you apprised on a regular basis. When an offer is made, your agent will typically and should contact you immediately. It is the agent's responsibility to inform you of any offers made and to help you determine if the offer is acceptable or not. You are not required to accept any offer, but you will able to consult with your agent as to whether the offer is the best for you. There are sometimes factors other than dollar amount that would make the choice of publisher advantageous to the success of the book. You may also be able to leverage a higher advance through your agent's skills at negotiation.

Your agent will give you access to the industry and will give you guidance in your choices. There is a mutually beneficial relationship that should be respectful on both ends. Agent and publisher time can often move even more slowly than God's time. Don't immediately drop an agent for not adjusting to your expectations. We recommend patience, as a good agent will tend to be busy. However, an agency contract should not tie you up for years. You should be able to terminate at will. You don't need to sign away your life just because you are eager to see your words in print.

Once you sign with an agent, don't turn "Hollywood." It's tempting to want to brag and show off. Do this all you want but on your own time. Don't mistake your agent for your employee. Here are some *dos* and *don'ts*:

- Do not call your agent so frequently that he feels he needs to be in a permanent "meeting."
- Do not obsess about the status of your book.
- Do go on with your life and try to believe that your existence does not depend on the publishing of your book.
- Do not bark orders to the support staff.
- Do butter up the support staff, as they can make or break you.
- Do not be temperamental.
- Do be willing to be flexible in the process of developing your project for submission.
- Do be willing to accept rejection.
- Do not blame your agent and take out a contract on his life.
- Do acknowledge your agent in all your published books.
- Do send presents (I added that!)—but don't feel obligated, as some agents don't like to feel beholden.

What If I Am Given an Offer by a Publishing House?

You know what to do—give thanks! Then get down to business. If you received the offer on your own, without benefit of an agent, contact any agents who turned you down, wave the offer under their noses, and say, "Would you like to represent me now?" This is not an exercise in spite but a strategy to enhance your negotiating presence with the publisher. Agents often negotiate publishing contracts for books they have not sold; you will wind up with an expert to oversee the contract negotiations and editorial process for you, and you will pay a smaller commission than if you had signed with an agent before finding a publisher. Another big advantage is that you have now obtained an agent who will potentially consider you for future projects.

Seriously consider trying to get an agent to help you negotiate your publishing contract. Your personal lawyer may not be the right person for this job. She may not be familiar with publishing contracts, and it is her role to find flaws, not to close deals. An agent, on the other hand, is there to craft a deal that's to your best advantage. The agent's fee is related to the amount of royalty income he can negotiate for you; he will want to see that the contract is weighted as heavily as possible in your favor and will try to retain appropriate subsidiary rights, such as audio or video productions that stem from your book.

Also, leave your "significant other" out of the process. Some writers have lost deals because they brought an overly exuberant, totally unsavvy, and nit-picking spouse into the contract negotiations. This situation can get very sticky for the publisher, and any bad past experiences with this sort of situation may make them want to run the other way.

The contract defines your commitments to the publishing house and its commitments to you. It includes such items as the deadline for the manuscript submission, approximate page length, the amount of your advance, your royalty percentage, and the retention and potential sale of subsidiary rights to your book. Resources for writers such as the Authors Guild (*authorsguild.org*) contain copies of publishing contracts that you can learn from. You will be able to see what terms are negotiable and what terms are simply not up for grabs. Even if you have an agent, educate yourself regarding publishing contracts.

Don't expect a big advance the first time around. By having a publisher, you have someone to make your book exist and someone who will help you launch it into the universe—and who is paying a lot of money to do it. Remember that bookstores sell books by consignment, and they can return unsold books to the publisher at any time. Without a sales history to estimate from, a publisher is taking a risk on a first-time writer, and a small advance—under $7,000—reflects that risk.

The sale of your spiritual manuscript is only the beginning of the publishing process. You will begin working with an editor who will critique your book and suggest changes. If you sold your book on proposal, you will be writing the book. Even if you have sold a completed manuscript, you are far from finished. As you learned in chapter 8, you'll be working with many members of the publisher's team. Expect that your final published text will look very different from your original manuscript. Accept that their input has value and enjoy your ride!

Why Did the Publisher Change My Title?

Titles are such a personal thing! They are so short and clever that authors often become more attached to them than to any other part of the text. But be warned—the publisher will very likely rename your book in order to meet the needs of the market. You may not agree, and you can fight, but in the end the publisher is usually right. If you truly hate their idea, go ahead and protest, but back up your protest with logic and reason. It's not enough to object because of pride of authorship.

Everything on the cover of the book is a form of advertising. The graphics are meant to create a mood and to entice readers to look inside. The title is intended to grab the attention of readers and convince them that there is something they need within the pages. Many books have endorsements from well-known writers or authorities in the field. If you believe you can obtain endorsements from prominent individuals, let your publisher know. Good endorsements are part of the entire advertising package. They will give your book credibility, and consumers will feel that it offers value to them.

Your Role in Publicity and Marketing

Promoting your book is a partnership between you and your publisher. No one, not even your publisher, knows your book as well as you do, and publishers have limited resources to promote books. Your publisher will be most active in the months immediately before and after your book's publication date, sending out galley copies and press releases to reviewers in hopes of getting your book reviewed or otherwise mentioned in print. After the book is in the stores, your publisher will likely set up book-signings at stores in your area or wherever you are able to travel. After those first crucial months, however, you are on your own. The publisher must turn their attention to the next season's titles. If you want your book to continue to move off the shelves, you have to put on your publicity hat.

Because the best advertising is word of mouth, you can generate buzz through speaking to groups and selling your book afterward, lining up bookstore readings on your own, querying newspaper or magazine editors about reviews or features based on facets of your book, or arranging local television or radio appearances.

If you are shy or have a humble personality, you will have to get over the fear of promoting yourself. This is where your hook comes in very handy. You'll use it and refine it even more to promote yourself to the media. This may burst your bubble of what publicity will be like, but producers and editors don't care about your book or that you are an author. All they want is a guest who will give them an entertaining show or a great story for their publication. Be careful not to overpromote yourself or your book to the media; they are not interested in your book per se or in you as a personality but only in how you can shine light on some current news events or trend. The crux of publicity is thinking like a television producer or magazine editor who is constantly looking for fresh material that will resonate with viewers or readers. If you can shift your perception from wanting to sell your book to wanting to create a marketable show or article that will answer their needs, you'll be successful at publicity. (See "Spirit-Friendly Resources" for information about publicity coaching.)

Your Choices as a Professional Spiritual Writer

Spirituality for many is a competitive business. We are not referring to the publishing industry; we are referring to spiritual people competing against others for a greater sense of importance. This attitude is prevalent in publishing especially since spirituality has become such a lucrative subject area. Some spiritual messengers have become the prophets of our day through the best-selling status of their books, and this is attractive to people who want all the material things this earth has to offer.

The messengers who are most sustaining are those who do not forget where the information comes from. There is nothing inherently wrong with become vastly successful with your writing. We hope this book helps you to do just that. You choose your path. You choose to be the messenger or the message. There are many opportunities for you and many professionals who will not care what direction you have chosen on your path and writer's journey. Keep in mind that it is up to you to maintain your integrity. Persist on your path with a sense of gratitude and humility, and you will already have achieved the greatest success that could be expected of anyone.

You will encounter obstacles on your path to publication just as would any writer. But know that the obstacles you encounter are perfect for your experience and be glad that they are there. In trying situations you are forced to reach for your inner resources; the most annoying situations or people can be the ones that help you grow the most. By trusting exactly what is in front of you, you will see that you are on the right path and that you are not alone.

Book publishing has its methods, and the spiritual path has its methods too. There are many things we can't control in either arena and shouldn't try to. But there are many things we can control and influence with our choices and by listening to the answers we are given. The answers are everywhere in equal proportion to the questions. You have learned to be connected to your inner spirit. Trust that and move ahead!

Part Four
SPIRIT-FRIENDLY RESOURCES

These agents and publishers have kindly identified themselves as understanding and appreciating spiritual material. However, be mindful that these are professionals and do not assume that because they are sensitive to your goals they are going to reduce their standards. They answer to their higher truth, but they also answer to the realities of the publishing industry. Apply your left-brain knowledge with your spirit. If you rise to the challenge given, you will have the potential to succeed. You will find that the agents and editors listed in this book are very special people. You will be blessed to work with them.

Though we have made every effort to ensure that the contact information following is complete and accurate, remember that in the ever-changing publishing community it will always be worth your while to call and double-check the address and the editor's or agent's name. The first section lists spirit-friendly agents. Read their entries carefully for hints regarding the type of material they represent. This listing is comprehensive but not complete. If you hear of another agent you'd like to query, call first to see if he or she represents spiritual material.

If you have decided not to work with an agent or are unable to find one to represent you, check out the second list of spirit-friendly publishing houses. These publishers, when possible, have been very specific about the types of submissions they want to see. Before you submit to them, familiarize yourself with their booklists and Web sites to make sure that your book would be a good fit. Unless they indicate that only agents should submit material, go for it!

Agents

This is a list of spirit-friendly agents—in other words, agents who have indicated an interest in spiritual material. These agents have been selected because they have a sincere interest in writers and the spiritual path, but this is meant to be a sampling rather than an exhaustive list. While this list will at least get you started, there are certainly more agents who will consider spiritual material—and all it takes to find them is a little research.

All agents are looking for material that can be commercially profitable. Remember that they are industry insiders with the experience to know what will sell and what will not. You should take their entries seriously. Many have shared their views on what "spirituality" means to them and how best to present your material as well as what they do not want to see. If they specify the kinds of material that they are and aren't interested in, respect their boundaries or you are wasting your—and their—time. These agents want to love your material, and they hope to find work that will not only make its way to the marketplace but that will have a positive impact on those who read it.

If an agent requests your manuscript after reading your query, be sure to send a copy of the original letter with your submission. It is difficult for agents, accustomed as they are to reviewing thousands of queries, to remember each one they request. It is to your advantage to remind them. Remember to include contact information as well. In your new cover letter, explain that your material was requested, who you are, what your background is, and what your credentials are. You should never miss an opportunity to persuade, but make your submission as simple as possible.

Make sure in any correspondence that you do not assume the agent knows who you are. It never hurts to repeat the contact information. It helps you build recognition with a potential agent by reminding him of conversations or previous correspondence. This courtesy is always appreciated and will show that you are the consummate professional. And whether it is specified or not, remember that if you want a response, you must always include an SASE—with enough postage!—with each query letter or submission. If an agency will consider e-mail queries, do not send any attachments, as most agencies will not open them.

Altair Literary Agency

141 Fifth Avenue, Suite 8N, New York, NY 10010 • 212-505-3320

The spirit-friendly agent at this agency is Andrea Pedolsky. Ms. Pedolsky is interested in the history of religion and new ideas about religion. This is not the same thing as fundamentalist treatises that are appropriate for a specifically Christian market. You should have a practice and/or have been published in the field about which you are writing. Previous books or articles are a plus. You should send a well-thought-out and carefully composed query letter, citing your related credentials. You may also submit a complete proposal.

Loretta Barrett Books, Inc.

101 Fifth Avenue, 11th floor, New York, NY 10003 • 212-242-3420

Loretta Barrett was an executive editor at Doubleday and has been a literary agent since 1990. Ms. Barrett is interested in spiritual material but not poetry. You should send a well-written query, providing background information on your writing, work, or experience. You may also submit a detailed marketing plan.

Hal Zina Bennett & Associates

9827 Irvine Avenue, Upper Lake, CA 95485

707-275-9011 • E-mail: *halbooks@saber.net*

Hal Z. Bennett offers both agenting and manuscript develop-
ment. He has been helping authors of spiritual books and health
books both develop and place their manuscripts for over thirty years.
His client list includes best-selling authors such as Shakti Gawain,
Jerry Jampolsky, M.D., Alexandra Kennedy, Cherie Carter-Scott,
Judith Orloff, M.D., Stanislav Grof, M.D., Mike Samuels, M.D.,
Leonard Laskow, M.D., Emmett Miller, M.D., and Susan Lark, M.D.
Three of his manuscript-development clients have been featured
on *Oprah*, including Dr. Phil McGraw. Please send a short query by
e-mail first.

Pam Bernstein & Associates, Inc.

790 Madison Avenue, Suite 310, New York, NY 10021

212-288-1700; fax: 212-288-3054

Pam Bernstein was with the William Morris Agency for fifteen
years. In 1993, she founded her own agency. Ms. Bernstein is interested
in quality spiritual material. Send a brief query explaining the work and
your background. Ms. Bernstein says she can't stress enough that you
should let go of unrealistic expectations about your advance and your
importance with your publisher. It takes time to build an author's career,
particularly in this area. Some examples of titles she has sold are *Recovery of Sacred Psychology* by Peter Rinehart (Addison-Wesley) and *Yoga
Baby* by Dr. DeAnson Parker (Broadway).

Daniel Bial Agency

41 West 83rd Street, Suite 5-C, New York, NY 10024 • 212-721-1786

Mr. Bial was an editor for fifteen years, including ten years at
HarperCollins. He founded his own agency in 1992.

Bleecker Street Associates, Inc.

532 LaGuardia Place, New York, NY 10012 • 212-677-4492

Agent Agnes Birnbaum spent sixteen years as an editor before starting her own agency in 1984. She was senior editor at Pocket Books and editor in chief of Award Books, later a part of Berkley. Ms. Birnbaum has an interest in New Age and spiritual material. You may contact her with a short letter about the book and your credentials for writing the book. She looks for writers with talent and creative new ideas. You should be passionate about your work and willing to self-promote. Educate yourself about the pros and cons of the business behind the books.

Book Ends, LLC

136 Long Hill Road, Gillette, NJ 07933

908-604-2652 • *www.bookends-inc.com*

Jacky Sach is interested in spiritual (rather than religious) material and accepts both mail and e-mail queries. Some categories include recovery, spiritual recovery, outside traditional religion, nature-based spirituality, animals and spirituality, as well as Wicca, Buddhism, eastern spirituality, yoga, Buddhism, and Tantra. She does not focus on religious aspects of traditional religions but is interested in the mystical or any type of spiritual quest—if the quality of the writing is good. She likes personal stories of change with some kind of redemptive quality but nothing dogmatic or prescriptive. Ms. Sach says that she has received submissions with very good ideas but the arrogance of the author's voice or the negativity that comes through defeats the purpose. Keep your letter short and be sure to include your relevant credentials. An example of one title she sold is *The Complete Idiot's Guide to Hinduism* by Linda Johnsen (Macmillan).

Jane Jordan Browne Multimedia Product Development, Inc.

410 South Michigan Avenue, Suite 724, Chicago, IL 60604

312-922-3063

Among its other genres, this house has had much success with Christian fiction, spirituality, and New Age material. They accept queries only by mail. They will not accept unsolicited manuscripts or proposals. For the Christian and inspirational markets their client list includes, among others, Francine Rivers, Lynn Coote, Johorne Schmidt, Anna Schmidt, and Dee Henderson. They place Christian books with such publishers as Zondervan, Tyndale, and Multnomah.

Pema Browne, Ltd.

Pine Road, HCR Box 104B, Neversink, NY 12765
914-985-2936 or 914-985-2062

This agency has been in business since 1966. Pema Browne (Pema rhymes with Emma) is a widely exhibited artist and painter. She is also an art buyer. Browne is interested in New Age, scholarly, and popular works in religion, spirituality, and reference. It is her belief that spiritual material is becoming more mainstream as a sign of the times. Browne is not interested in books on astrology or the occult. Well-written proposals by qualified authors will gain her attention. Browne also looks for authors who show integrity and professionalism and who continue to polish their skills. A title that has done well for this agency is *Healing the Trauma of Past Lives* by Thelma Freedman, Ph.D. (Citadel Press).

Clausen, Mays & Tahan Literary Agency

249 West 34th Street, New York, NY 10001
212-239-4343 • E-mail: *cmtassist@aol.com*

Mary M. Tahan looks for authors who have a vision, are willing to listen to constructive suggestions, and will promote aggressively. She does not categorize herself in terms of religious, inspirational, New Age, or spiritual but rather looks for individual authors who resonate with her. Though she's a traditional Christian, the books that she represents do not need to conform specifically to Christian beliefs. She looks for books that are not extreme, condemnatory, or exclusionary. The kind of spirituality books that she thinks are publishable are broad and do not dictate beliefs. Examples of books she admires are those by Marianne Williamson and M Scott Peck. Not only are they good writers, but they take complicated material and make it accessible through personal anecdotes. She will not represent angry, negative, or preachy books. You should send a well-written query letter, including an author bio. You may also include a brief proposal.

Liza Dawson Associates

240 West 35th Street, New York, NY 10001 • 212-465-9071

Liza Dawson was an editor at Pocket Books, an editor at William Morrow, and an executive editor and vice president of G. P. Putnam. Ms. Dawson is interested in spiritual (but not New Age) work by credentialed authors. She looks for writers who have a deep knowledge of their area of expertise and an ability to follow through on commitments. It also helps if you are an entertaining conversationalist.

Sandra Dijkstra Literary Agency

PMB 515, 1155 Camino Del Mar, Del Mar, CA 92014-2605
858-755-3115, ext. 18 • E-mail: *sdla@dijkstraagency.com*

After working as a university professor, Sandra Dijkstra became a literary agent. She is interested in new and exciting material in spirituality if it is supported by relevant credentials and experience in the field addressed in the proposal. She does not seek books that reflect a personal journey through memoir. Ms. Dijkstra suggests that a writer first find a bookseller, author, or publisher to recommend them. Her agency reviews queries but will not look at unsolicited manuscripts. She recommends that writers try to publish their work in magazines. Dijkstra particularly looks for books that contribute to the basic well-being of humanity and spiritual books with a practical application.

ForthWrite Literary Agency
23852 West Pacific Coast Highway #701, Malibu, CA 90265
310-456-5698

Wendy Keller has been an agent since 1988 and founded ForthWrite in 1989. She is interested in the metaphysical and in perennial wisdom. Query first.

Sarah Jane Freymann Literary Agency
59 West 71st Street, Suite 9B, New York, NY 10023 • 212-362-9277

Sarah Jane Freymann has been a literary agent since the 1970s and represents an eclectic list that reflects her many interests and her willingness to be seduced by wonderful books. She observes that authors who are genuinely grounded in their spiritual practice are the best able to maintain a healthy perspective. You may contact Ms. Freymann with a query letter. No phone calls, please.

The Jeff Herman Agency, LLC
332 Bleecker St., Suite G31, New York, NY 10014
212-941-0540; fax: 212-941-0614
E-mail: *jeff@jeffherman.com* • *www.jeffherman.com*

The Jeff Herman Agency specializes in most areas of adult non-fiction with a strong interest in spirituality, self-help, how-to, popular psychology, and popular business.

Natasha Kern Literary Agency, Inc.
P.O. Box 2908, Portland, OR 97208-2908
E-mail: *nkla@teleport.com* • *www.natashakern.com*

This agency represents New Age, inspirational, alternative health, and spirituality (both fiction and nonfiction). In fiction, she looks for novels from any genre—literary or mainstream fiction, mystery, romance, or science fiction—with characters whose spiritual beliefs inform the work. Books of this nature that she has represented include *The Skull Mantra* by Eliot Pattison, *Daughter of God* by Lew Perdue, and *The Forgiving Hour* by Robin Lee Hatcher.

In nonfiction, Ms. Kern looks for books from all spiritual traditions including Native American, Buddhist, Christian, Jewish, New Age, Wiccan, and other beliefs or practices including those that are idiosyncratic to the author. She is interested in books with something new to say, that are primarily ecumenical, and that inspire the reader. Some of her most successful nonfiction books are *Aphrodite's Daughters* by Jalaja Bonheim and *Daughters of Dignity: African Women in the Bible and the Virtues of Black Womanhood* by LaVerne McCain Gill. She is not looking for books that proselytize or prescribe rules and practices. Send queries by mail only.

Literary Management Group

P.O. Box 680758, Franklin, TN 37068-0758

E-mail: *brb@brucebarbour.com*

This agency represents exclusively Christian, motivational, and inspirational material and specializes in evangelical Christian literature including fiction, nonfiction, gift books, and children's. Submissions not based on historical orthodox Christianity will automatically be returned. They generally pass on first fiction, poetry, and short stories. They have been most successful with business books with Christian themes, prayer, contemporary fiction, deeper spiritual insights (rather than light inspirations), self-help, unconventional ministry application, and devotionals.

Toni Lopopolo Literary Management

8837 School House Lane, Coopersburg, PA 18036

215-679-0560 • E-mail: *lopopolobooks@aol.com*

Agent Toni Lopopolo has worked for Bantam Books, Houghton Mifflin, Macmillan, and St. Martin's Press, and she has been an agent since 1990. Ms. Lopopolo believes that we "graduate" to new levels from where we landed as young people in our respective religious upbringings. She presently represents *The Twelve Spiritual Temperaments*. She looks for spiritual material from writers who have credentials and platform.

Linda Roghaar Literary Agency, Inc.

133 High Point Drive, Amherst, MA 01002

413-256-1921 • E-mail: *lroghaar@aol.com* • *www.lindaroghaar.com*

Linda L. Roghaar has worked in publishing since 1974, first in bookstores and then as a publisher's sales rep. She established her agency in 1997. Ms. Roghaar is looking for quality spiritual material including New Age, religion, Christian, and Judaica. Christian refers to liberal, nonexclusive Christian or scholarly work. Ms. Roghaar looks for material that is well-grounded and authentic. She stays away from narrative descriptions of a spiritual quest as well as narrative fiction. Some representative titles include *A Place Like Any Other* by Molly Wolf (Doubleday) and *Living Faith Day by Day* by Debra Farrington (Penguin/Putnam/Perigee).

Ms. Roghaar makes many of her decisions on a book-by-book basis, finding that when she tries to exclude a particular genre she inevitably comes across a book on the subject that she loves. Visit her Web site to learn more about her tastes. Ms. Roghaar is turned off by queries from authors who hint that it's sure to be a best-seller but do not specify what they are writing about. Send queries and a complete proposal.

Rita Rosenkranz Literary Agency

440 West End Avenue, #15D, New York, NY 10024 • 212-873-6333

Rita Rosenkranz is a former editor with major New York houses, and she founded Rita Rosenkranz Literary Agency in 1989. She is interested in spiritual and inspirational titles that will appeal to mainstream houses (i.e., no specialized niches such as witchcraft). A representative title is

My Mother's Charms: Timeless Gifts of Family Wisdom by Kathleen Oldford (HarperSanFrancisco). Send queries by mail.

Writers House, LLC
21 West 26th Street, New York, NY 10010
212-685-2400; fax: 212-685-1781

The spirit-friendly agent at this well-established agency is Karen Solem. She prefers to be contacted by mail or fax. She will not accept e-mail submissions. She is interested in a broad spectrum of spiritual subjects. She makes the determination to take on a spiritual book in the same way she makes decisions on secular work. She says she needs to love the material and must have a vision for the project and the client before she will consider if she thinks it can be successful. Ms. Solem has sold women's fiction and an African-American series, and she has represented works to the Christian Booksellers Association.

Publishers

To help you jump-start your search for a publisher, the listings that follow are representative of the thousands of publishers who handle spiritual material. Most have Web sites that provide more detailed information about the types of books they publish and the specific information they look for from prospective authors. Use this list as inspiration and motivation to take your manuscript to the far-flung reaches of the publishing world!

Abingdon Press
201 Eighth Avenue South, Nashville, TN 37202-0801
615-749-6451 • *www.abingdon.org*

Abingdon Press is a division of the United Methodist Publishing House, founded in 1789. It publishes both scholarly books and books for the popular religious market. Send queries to Mary Catherine Dean, editor of trade books for Abingdon. Ms. Dean looks for books that help people and families live Christian lives or that have Christian relevance in areas such as personal meditation, faith enrichment, and encouragement.

Abingdon's Dimension for Living imprint focuses on practical Christian living. It looks for manuscripts that "Celebrate life and affirm Christian faith." Sally Sharpe is the editor.

American Federation of Astrologers

P.O. Box 22040, Tempe, AZ 85285-2040

480-838-1751 • *www.astrologers.com*

Unlike most other publishers, AFA considers only completed manuscripts, preferably with a disk. AFA looks for astrological books that relate to daily life. It works only with credentialed astrologers. Recent titles show astrology's application to business and health. AFA also offers home courses in astrology and membership newsletters. Its mission is to promote an understanding of astrology for the betterment of people's lives.

Andrews McMeel Universal

4520 Main Street, Suite 700, Kansas City, MO 64111

816-932-6700 • *www.uexpress.com*

Andrews McMeel publishes many types of commercial trade nonfiction books, including New Age and inspirational. While it does not accept unsolicited or unagented manuscripts, you may query Chris Schillig, vice president and editorial director.

Jason Aronson Publishers

230 Livingston Street, Northvale, NJ 07647

201-767-4093 • *www.aronson.com*

Jason Aronson publishes books of Jewish interest and traditional Judaica. It will consider both scholarly and popular books. Send queries to Arthur Kurzweil, editor in chief.

Astro Communications Services

5521 Ruffin Road, San Diego, CA 92123 • *www.astrocom.com*

Astro Communications publishes books both for the serious student or the practitioner of astrology and for general audiences interested in astrology and in improving life through its application. Address queries and proposals to Maritha Pottenger, editorial director.

Augsburg Fortress Publishers

P.O. Box 1209, Minneapolis, MN 55440-1209

612-330-3300 • *www.augsburgfortress.org*

Augsburg Fortress is the publishing house of the Evangelical Lutheran Church in America. It looks for books that appeal to mainstream religious readers. Its list includes books on biblical studies, theology, pastoral care, ministry, African-American studies, church history, spirituality, life issues, and children's books, as well as music and education resources for pre-school through adult. Direct queries to Robert Klausmeier.

Aurora Press

300 Catron Road, Suite B, Santa Fe, NM 87501 • 505-989-9804

Aurora specializes in astrology, metaphysics, and global consciousness. Its books are catalysts for personal growth, balance, and transformation and help the reader integrate ancient wisdom with today's daily life. Aurora publishes just a few books each year and looks for ideas that are fresh, practical, and helpful to people as they explore their inner potential, expand their consciousness, or improve the quality of their lives. Unsolicited manuscripts are not accepted. Send queries to Barbara Somerfield, president, or Michael King, director.

Avalon Publishing Group

161 William Street, 16th floor, New York, NY 10038

646-375-2570 • *www.avalonpub.com*

Avalon's imprint Marlowe & Company publishes books on spirituality, religion, personal growth, self-help, and wellness. Send queries to managing editor Matthew Lore.

Baker Book House

P.O. Box 6287, Grand Rapids, MI 49516-6287

616-676-9185 • *www.bakerbooks.com*

Baker Book House is a Christian publisher with an ecumenical Protestant perspective. Its Revell imprint publishes nonfiction books of general interest that relate Christian living to today's world, such as contemporary issues, women's issues, parenting, and single life. Revell also looks for good Christian fiction (that is, fiction with a Christian theme that is gripping and relevant to Christian readers). New writers are welcome. No science fiction, end times, satanic issues, or issue-oriented fiction (such as abortion or creationism). It avoids books that overtly proselytize, and it seeks books that speak to the heart. Contact Lonnie Hull Dupont.

Ballantine Publishing Group

1540 Broadway, New York, NY 10036

212-782-9800 • *www.randomhouse.com*

Ballantine is a publishing group under the Random House umbrella that publishes commercial fiction and nonfiction. One of its editors, JoAnn Wycoff, acquires serious books on religion and Judeo-Christian history. She prefers nondenominational material that can appeal to a wide audience, which excludes such topics as the afterlife and New Age concepts. She is not interested in Bible-based books written by lay people or literal interpretations of the Bible by clergy. She will consider serious biography, especially books about spiritual quests, but it must be exceptional. The quest itself is almost less important to her than the quality of writing. The writer must have outstanding storytelling and writing skills to compete in this area. Only agented submissions are accepted.

Bantam Dell Publishing Group

1540 Broadway, New York, NY 10036

212-782-9000 • *www.randomhouse.com/bantamdell*

Bantam Dell is a publishing group under the Random House umbrella of companies. Query Toni Burbank with spiritual, New Age, and religious material. She is not interested in anything that reflects someone's personal quest or philosophy, for example, books about the author's spiritual perspective based on his experiences. She is particularly interested in titles regarding Buddhism and all things Eastern. She will do some mainstream Christian books, such as Mary Morrisey's *Building Your Field of Dreams*, a book about Jesus but for a mainstream audience. She is not looking for anything too scholarly. Bantam Dell accepts unsolicited queries with a one-page author biography attached.

Barricade Books, Inc.

185 Bridge Plaza North, Suite 308A, Fort Lee, NJ 07024

201-944-7600 • *www.barricadebooks.com*

Barricade Books specializes in books that other houses consider too controversial, such as New Age, occult, and spiritual titles. Send queries to Carole Stuart, publisher.

Beacon Press

25 Beacon Street, Boston, MA 02108 • 617-742-2110 • *www.beacon.org*

Beacon was established in 1854 by the Unitarian Universalist Association, which fosters the intellectual celebration of life and spirit. Unitarians embrace the concept of one God experienced through many different traditions: Jewish, Buddhist, Christian, and so forth. Beacon's list reflects this perspective with an extensive Jewish-studies series and books on sufism, yoga, and Buddhism. Beacon looks for nonfiction books that deal with the search for truth and meaning, world religions, and practical spirituality (in other words, spirituality in everyday lives). It rarely publishes memoirs. Send queries only (no manuscripts) to Tisha Hooks. She likes a straightforward, concise, and thorough query that addresses all the major points discussed in chapter 10 of this book.

Bear & Company Publishing

See Inner Traditions.

Bethany House Publishers

11400 Hampshire Avenue South, Bloomington, MN 55438
612-829-2500 • *www.bethanyhouse.com*

Bethany House publishes fiction and nonfiction books with evangelical Christian themes. Its credo is "God's light shining through good books." The editors are interested in devotional books, books about relationships and family, and books with biblical references. Bethany also has a strong list for young people. See the Web site for submission guidelines and send queries to Sharon Madison, acquisitions editor.

Beyond Words Publishing, Inc.

20827 N.W. Cornell Road, Suite 500, Hillsboro, OR 97124
503-531-8700 • *www.beyondword.com*

The mission of Beyond Words is to publish books that "Inspire to Integrity." In addition to children's and coffee-table books, Beyond Words publishes approximately twelve nonfiction titles per year on topics such as practical spirituality, parenting, personal growth, and human's kinship with nature. It does not publish fiction, poetry, devotionals, memoirs, or workbooks, even those on spiritual topics. See the Web site for submission guidelines and send queries or proposals to Jenefer Angell, acquisitions editor, adult division.

Broadway Books
1540 Broadway, New York, NY 10036

212-782-9000 • *www.randomhouse.com*

Broadway Books is a division of Random House. It looks for high-quality, unique books with strong marketability by authors who are either an authority on the topic or whose research and arguments are based on more than just their own opinion. Contact either Ann Campbell or Lauren Marino, both of whom have an interest in books on spirituality.

Career Press
See New Page Books.

Celestial Arts
P.O. Box 7123, Berkeley, CA 94707

510-559-1600 • *www.celestialarts.com*

Celestial Arts, an imprint of Ten Speed Press, publishes books that will "change your life." The easy-to-use Web site details the numerous spiritual titles on its list; Celestial Arts also publishes books on, among other diverse topics, creativity, healing, women's issues, inspiration, death, and Wiccan issues. See the Web site for submission guidelines.

Conari Press
2550 Ninth Street, Suite 101, Berkeley, CA 94710

510-649-7190 • *www.conari.com*

The mission of Conari Books is to be a catalyst for change. It publishes books on relationships, women's issues, sexuality, relationships, and spirituality. Conari looks for authors with integrity who write what they believe in and not what they think will sell. Address queries to Claudia Schaav and Mary Jane Ryan.

Contemporary Books

P.O. Box 182625, Columbus, OH 43218

877-226-4997 • *www.contemporarybooks.com*

Contemporary is a division of McGraw Hill Companies. Contact Peter Hoffman and Linda Gray.

Cook Communications Ministries

4050 Lee Vance View, Colorado Springs, CO 80918

www.cookministries.com

Cook Communications is a publisher of mainstream Christian books. Its mission is to encourage Christians to develop a greater understanding of the Bible and to apply Christian values in everyday life. Each of its imprints follows the same theme of linking church with home and life: Chariot Books seeks to reach young people and children, fostering their spiritual development by training them in and through the family to be disciples of Christ. Lion Publishing publishes trade books for seekers who have not necessarily been evangelized. Victor Books looks for books for adults that cover all relevant subjects of spirituality, Christian philosophy, and social issues as they relate to life in Christ. Queries should be directed to Melissa Borger.

Cross Cultural Publications, Inc.

P.O. Box 506, Notre Dame, IN 46556

219-273-6526 • *www.crossculturalpub.com*

This house publishes five to twenty titles each year with the goal of promoting interfaith and cross-cultural understanding. It looks for spiritual and religious topics that are intellectually balanced and presented without judgment. It will consider poetry and likes books that explore new areas of thought. Credentials are important. Send queries and proposals to Cyriac Pullapilly.

The Crossing Press

1201 Shaffer Road, Suite B, Santa Cruz, CA 95060

831-420-1110 • *www.crossingpress.com*

The Crossing Press publishes books on natural and alternative healing, empowerment, personal growth and transformation, and spirituality. It also has an interest in feminism, the men's movement, and gay and lesbian issues. It no longer publishes fiction, poetry, or calendars. The Crossing Press welcomes both queries and proposals that include a detailed outline, sample chapter, and marketing plan. See the Web site for detailed submission instructions.

Crossroad Publishing Company

481 Eighth Avenue, Suite 1550, New York, NY 10001

212-868-1801 • E-mail: *kevindicamillo@crossroadpublishing.com*

Crossroad publishes books on spirituality, religious studies, world religions, and theology for the general and popular religious markets. It is an entrepreneurial house that vigorously supports its products. Call or e-mail for catalog and submission guidelines. Crossroad will accept unagented and unsolicited submissions.

Crossway Books

1300 Crescent Street, Wheaton, IL 60187-5883

630-682-4300 • *www.crosswaybooks.org*

Crossway is a division of Good News Publishers. It publishes fiction and nonfiction books that have an evangelical perspective and purpose and that combine God's word with the inspiration to carry it out. Crossway publishes for both a religious and a general market and will accept books with an issue orientation. Send queries with a one- to two-page double-spaced synopsis and up to two chapters to Marvin Padgett, vice president, editorial.

Crown Publishing Group

299 Park Avenue, New York, NY 10171

212-751-2600 • *www.randomhouse.com*

Crown is a division of Random House. Its imprint Harmony Books publishes spiritual and inspirational titles. Harmony is not interested in New Age subjects but rather topics of practical spirituality and self-help. Send queries to Harmony's editorial director Linda Lowenthal.

Doubleday & Company, Inc.

1540 Broadway, New York, NY 10036

212-782-9000 • *www.randomhouse.com*

Doubleday was founded in 1897. Today it is a division of Random House, and it publishes mainstream nonfiction books, including some spiritual titles. Eric Major, Director of Religious Publishing, looks for scholarly religious works and books on spirituality and controversial subjects. Major also seeks books on religions, including Buddhism, Hinduism, and Judaica.

Dutton Plume

375 Hudson Street, New York, NY 10014

212-366-2000 • *www.penguinputnam.com*

Dutton, an imprint of Penguin Putnam, is a mainstream publisher responsible for titles such as *Reaching to Heaven: A Spiritual Journey through Life and Death* by James Van Praagh. Dutton prefers and will likely accept only agented submissions. However, you can direct queries for spiritual and religious subjects to Brian Tart, editor in chief, who acquires books in the areas of self-help and spirituality.

Wm. B. Eerdmans Publishing Company

255 Jefferson Avenue Southeast, Grand Rapids, MI 49503

1-800-253-7521 • *www.eerdmans.com*

Wm. B. Eerdmans is a major independent Catholic and Protestant publisher. Its books offer a Christian perspective on topics as diverse as anthropology, music, social issues, and many others. It publishes both academic and popular market titles. Contact Jon Pott, editor in chief.

Feldheim Publishers

202 Airport Executive Park, Nanuet, NY 10954

845-356-2282 • *www.feldheim.com*

Feldheim is a leading publisher of Jewish material. It looks for significant works of Orthodox Jewish thought as well as more popular titles of practical interest to its readers. Query letters should be directed to Yitzchak Feldheim, president.

Gibbs Smith

P.O. Box 667, Layton, UT 84041

801-544-9800 • *www.gibbs-smith.com*

Gibbs Smith publishes general trade nonfiction books and has as its mission to "Enrich and inspire humankind." Its editors look for a sense of passion and great purpose in a manuscript. Gibbs Smith operates out of a barn in the Rocky Mountains and prides itself on being resourceful. It looks to writers to be resourceful as well. Gail Yngve is the editor for New Age and inspirational.

Gospel Light

2300 Knoll Drive, Ventura, CA 93003

1-800-446-7735 • *www.gospellight.com*

Gospel Light specializes in publishing books on evangelism, discipleship, and Christian education. It looks for books that relate to people awakening to or renewing faith. Send queries to Kyle Duncan.

Hachai Publishing

156 Chester Avenue, Brooklyn, NY 11218

718-633-0100 • *www.hachai.com*

Each year, this house publishes about six children's titles relating to Jewish values. Books should show the relevance of the Torah in making positive choices. It looks for books on observance and contemporary Jewish life as well as biographies of significant men and women in Jewish history. Send queries to Dina Rosenfeld. Hachai purchases books outright, with no author advances or royalties offered.

Hampton Roads Publishing Company, Inc.

1125 Stoney Ridge Road, Charlottesville, VA 22902

804-296-2772 • *www.hrpub.com*

Hampton Roads publishes alternative medicine, visionary fiction, metaphysics, and young spirit (spiritual content for children). According to chief editor Frank DeMarco, Hampton Roads prefers books that present practical material which helps people develop themselves in real life. It looks for books that balance the left brain with the right.

Hampton Roads, pioneers in visionary fiction, also publishes novels that include themes of spirituality, metaphysics, past-life recall, or anything paranormal. Although this genre is in its early years, Hampton Roads will consider manuscripts of this kind to accommodate its growing list. It believes that visionary fiction is important because it engages the emotional and mental body at the same time, which leads to real change. Richard Leviton is the senior editor. He also looks for books that include the spiritual underpinnings of alternative health.

HarperCollins

353 Sacramento Street, Suite 500, San Francisco, CA 94111

415-477-4400 • *www.harpercollins.com*

This house is the leading religious trade publisher in the United States, publishing across all religious traditions. It looks for books to inspire the body, mind, and spirit. The house interests are diverse, including mysticism, Native American studies, spiritual journeys, philosophy, New Age, Gnosticism, Judaica, and any titles that can help readers on the path to self-awareness. HarperCollins does not accept unagented submissions.

Harvest House Publishers

1075 Arrowsmith, Eugene, OR 97402-9197

541-343-0123 • *www.harvesthousepubl.com*

Harvest House publishes nonfiction and fiction from a nondenominational, evangelical Christian perspective. Its goal is to help people be spiritually strong. It looks for a wide variety of subjects including Christian living, politics, parenting, inspiration, and spiritual growth. Its fiction covers romance, occult thrillers, mysteries, suspense, and Bible-based stories. It looks for high-quality writing and a topic that has relevance to Christian readers. Direct queries to the Manuscript Coordinator.

Hazelden Publishing Group

P.O. Box 176, Center City, MN 55012-0176

651-257-4010 • *www.hazelden.org*

Hazelden is a nonprofit publisher. By its own admission, Hazelden does not have the sophistication to attract major best-selling writers, but many of its books, such as *Codependent No More* by Melodie Beatie, have sold millions of copies worldwide. Hazelden publishes books based on addiction, recovery, and all subjects related to the constellation of family issues. Spirituality is a major underlying theme. It will consider memoirs, but it is not interested in dark stories that do not educate or have a positive impact on the reader. Hazelden relies solely on agents for submissions. Send queries to Rebecca Post, editorial director.

Henry Holt and Company

115 West 18th Street, New York, NY 10011

212-886-9200 • *www.henryholt.com*

Henry Holt is a mainstream publisher with a broad nonfiction list that runs the spectrum of subjects. It publishes books on philosophy, spirituality, and awareness. Direct queries to the Editorial Director.

Humanics Publishing Group

P.O. Box 7400, Atlanta, GA 30357

404-874-2176 • *www.humanicspub.com*

This house has a specialty in personal growth, relationships, philosophy, self-help, the environment, and a peaceful world. A major emphasis is also on Taoism, which is represented in a series devoted to the topic. Send queries to Arthur Bligh, acquisitions editor.

Inner Ocean Publishing, Inc.

P.O. Box 1239, Makawao, HI 96768-1239

808-573-8000 • *www.innerocean.com*

Inner Ocean is an intimate and selective small press whose mission is to publish books that help "create common goals for humanity, particularly as they relate to bringing better communication and peaceful coexistence, readers evolve as more conscious and purposeful beings." Inner Ocean is particularly interested in books on conscious business, personal growth, sacred travel, shamanism, personal growth, inspiration, and spiritual journeys. See the Web site for submission guidelines.

Inner Traditions/Bear & Company

P. O. Box 388, Rochester, VT 05767

802-767-3174 • *www.innertraditions.com*

Inner Traditions publishes books on alternative health that combine contemporary thought with the great healing traditions. It recently merged with Bear & Company, which has published books about intuition, channeling, herbs, and crystals, as well as books and products related to Native American spirituality, such as its illustrated Native American Medicine Cards. Inner Traditions/Bear looks for books with new perspectives on practical spirituality, self-transformation, and metaphysics. Its books are meant not only to heal and enlighten readers but to celebrate and heal the earth.

Innisfree Press

136 Roumfort Road, Philadelphia, PA 19119-1632

215-247-4085 • *www.innisfreepress.com*

Innisfree is an ecumenical publishing house named for the Yeats poem "Isle of Innisfree," and it publishes spiritual nonfiction classics "that call to the deep heart's core." Innisfree publishes about six titles per year, all with tender loving care and full involvement of the writer every step of the way. Publisher Marcia Broucek is open to seeing proposals in addition to queries. Innisfree looks for books that are practical, can be used by individuals or groups, and which pose more questions than answers. Innisfree does not accept poetry, children's books, fiction, or survival stories, nor does it publish New Age books.

Jewish Publication Society

2100 Arch Street, 2nd floor, Philadelphia, PA 19103

215-832-0600 • E-mail: *gbrown@jewishpub.org* • *www.jewishpub.org*

The Jewish Publication Society is the oldest English-language publisher of Jewish literature. Its titles aim to further Jewish culture and education. E-mail for manuscript submission information.

H. J. Kramer, Inc.

P.O. Box 1082, 102 Red Hill Circle, Tiburon, CA 94920
415-435-5367

Kramer's mission is to touch as many lives as possible with a message of hope for a better world through books that touch the heart and open the reader to spirit. It publishes metaphysical, religious, spiritual, self-help, and children's topics. Send queries to the Submissions Editor.

Leisure Books

276 Fifth Avenue, Suite 1008, New York, NY 10001
212-725-8811 • *www.dorchesterpub.com*

Leisure publishes books that combine paranormal concepts with romance. It likes books with werewolves, vampires, ghosts, and psychic phenomena as long as the main focus is the romance. Interested authors can send a query, three- to seven-page synopsis, and the first three chapters addressed to the Editorial Director.

Liguori Publications

One Liguori Drive, Liguori, MO 63057-9999
636-464-2500 • *www.liguori.org*

Liguori's Triumph Books imprint takes an ecumenical approach to the religious trade market. It seeks a wide readership through books that demonstrate a strong practical application in the fields of spirituality, inspiration, awareness, theology, and Christian living. Triumph will also publish books that are contemporary and controversial. Direct a proposal, outline, and two chapters to Judy Bauer, managing editor.

Llewellyn Worldwide, Ltd.

P.O. Box 64383, St. Paul, MN 55164-0383

651-291-1970 • *www.llewellyn.com*

Llewellyn was established in 1897 and is well-known for its large and diverse list of New Age, metaphysical, occult, healing, and spiritual books. Its books are practical and encourage expansion of readers' understanding of the universe of mind and spirit. Llewellyn asks that prospective authors read and follow its detailed submission guidelines, which are posted on the Web site.

Lotus Light Publications

P.O. Box 325, Twin Lakes, WI 53181

262-889-8561 • *www.lotuspress.com*

Lotus Light publishes books in the areas of health, yoga, Native American topics, philosophy and spirituality, metaphysics, and New Age topics. Send queries to Cathy Hoselton.

Mesorah Publications, Ltd.

4401 Second Avenue, Brooklyn, NY 11232

718-921-9000 • *www.artscroll.com*

Mesorah publishes for an Orthodox Jewish audience. Its books are as diverse as most mainstream publishers but within the parameters of Judaism. Mesorah publishes fiction and nonfiction, including biography, children's and juvenile, coffee-table books, cookbooks, gift books, reference, self-help, philosophy, spirituality, creative nonfiction, parenting, and more. Queries, proposals, or completed manuscripts may be sent to Mrs. D. Schechter.

Moody Press

820 North LaSalle Boulevard, Chicago, IL 60610

312-329-2101 • *www.moodypress.org*

Moody is an evangelical Christian publisher that serves as the publishing ministry of Moody Bible Institute. Its goal is to educate Christians and to provide evangelical materials for the non-Christians in the Christian person's life. It also publishes books that are true to biblical principles but that cover mainstream areas such as relationships and business. Moody publishes fiction as well. Direct query letters to Jim Bell.

Multnomah Publishers

P.O. Box 1720, Sisters, OR 97759

541-549-1144 • *www.multnomahbooks.com*

Multnomah is a Christian publisher with two imprints, Multnomah Press and Questar Books. Multnomah publishes books about Christian living, the family, and inspiration, while Questar focuses on a Christian perspective in self-awareness, self-improvement, theology, and popular fiction. Unagented queries, proposals, and manuscripts are not accepted; however, Multnomah expects, in the future, that it will accept on-line queries. It will accept queries made through appointment with Multnomah editors at writers' conferences they attend.

Thomas Nelson, Inc.

P.O. Box 141000, Nashville, TN 37214-1000

1-800-933-9673 • *www.thomasnelson.com*

The mission of Thomas Nelson is "To grow through fairness and integrity in distinctive service to all." It publishes, produces, and markets products that honor God and serve humanity. Its large list includes nonfiction titles on health, inspiration, self-help, psychology, family, parenting, and spirituality, as well as fiction from a Christian perspective. Thomas Nelson does not accept unagented queries, proposals, and manuscripts.

New Hope Publishers

P.O. Box 12065, Birmingham, AL 35202-2065

205-991-8100 • *www.newhopepubl.com*

This house is a division of the Woman's Missionary Union. New Hope publishes books related to Christian ethical issues and spiritual growth. Its titles address spiritual issues related to women, mission work, and guiding children in the Christian faith. Send queries to Jennifer Law, editor.

New Leaf Press

P.O. Box 726, Green Forest, AR 72638

1-800-999-3777 • *www.newleafpress.net*

New Leaf is a Christian publisher of titles on subjects including Christian living, prophecy, biography, theology, applied Christianity, history, Bible study, family, home, and marriage. New Leaf also publishes devotional works and books for evangelism. Send query letters to Jim Fletcher.

New Page Books

P.O. Box 687, Franklin Lakes, NJ 07417

1-800-227-3371 • *www.newpagebooks.com*

New Page is an imprint of Career Press. It publishes trade nonfiction on health, New Age, parenting, and psychology topics. Its excellent submission guidelines offer advice and detailed information. New Page prefers proposals for completed manuscripts. Send queries and proposals to Michael Lewis, acquisitions editor.

New World Library

14 Pamaron Way, Novato, CA 94949 • *www.newworldlibrary.com*

New World Library is dedicated to publishing quality books and cassettes that inspire and challenge people to improve the quality of their lives and our world. It focuses on spirituality, self-improvement, healthy cooking, parenting, women's studies, alternative health, religion, enlightened business, and multicultural studies. Address manuscripts to the Submissions Editor.

Onjinjinkta Publishing

909 Southeast Everett Mall Way, Suite A120, Everett, WA 98208
425-290-7809 • *www.onjinjinkta.com*

Onjinjinkta was created by Betty Eadie, the best-selling author of *Embraced by the Light*, the groundbreaking book about near-death experiences. While the house publishes general trade books, it is particularly strong in the area of spirituality. It prefers fiction that tends to enlighten. Direct queries to Peter Orullian, editor, or Tom Eadie, publisher.

Paragon House Publishers

2700 University Avenue West, Suite 200, Saint Paul, MN 55114-1016
651-644-3087 • *www.paragonhouse.com*

Paragon House publishes books in the areas of general philosophy, ethics, contemporary values, religion, women's studies, spirituality, and New Age topics. It publishes trade books, scholarly research, and textbooks. Laureen Enright is acquisitions editor.

Paulist Press

997 Macarthur Boulevard, Mahwah, NJ 07430
1-800-218-1903 • *www.paulistpress.com*

Paulist Press publishes ecumenical theology, Roman Catholic studies, and other nonfiction titles on spirituality, faith and culture, and personal growth. Some titles are provocative in areas of religious thought. It does not accept poetry. See the Web site for submission guidelines.

The Pilgrim Press

700 Prospect Avenue, Cleveland, OH 44115-1100

216-736-3764 • *www.pilgrimpress.com*

Pilgrim Press is part of the book-publishing arm of the United Church of Christ. This imprint is geared toward the inspirational market and looks for books that have the potential to make a difference. The Pilgrim Press publishes books on ethics, relationships, sexuality (including feminist as well as gay and lesbian issues), and activist spirituality. Direct query letters to Lynn Deming, publisher.

Presbyterian Publishing Corporation

100 Witherspoon Street, Louisville, KY 40202-1396

502-569-5000 • *www.ppcpub.org*

Presbyterian Publishing Corporation's Westminster John Knox Press is an imprint that publishes general-interest religious trade books on spirituality and personal growth as well as books that provide practical assistance for the family's revitalization. Send queries to managing editor Stephanie Egnotovich.

The Putnam Berkley Group

375 Hudson Street, New York, NY 10014

212-366-2000 • *www.penguinputnam.com*

Perigee Books, a trade paperback imprint of Penguin Putnam, publishes books on spiritual topics. Send queries related to spirituality to Jennifer Repo.

Red Wheel/Weiser

368 Congress Street, Boston, MA 02210

617-542-1324 • *www.redwheelweiser.com*

Weiser is interested in books about self-transformation, alternative healing, meditations, metaphysics, self-help, spirituality, Kabbalah,

Eastern religions, Buddhism, Earth religions, and anything that leads readers to find the path that is right for them. Weiser looks for books where the writer has something original to say. Send queries to the Editorial Department.

Rodale Press

33 East Minor Street, Emmaus, PA 18098-0099

610-967-5171 • *www.rodalepress.com*

Rodale Press is well-known for *Prevention Magazine* but also has a significant reputation in publishing books on health as well as practical spirituality. Its mission is to help people use the power of their bodies and minds to make their lives better. Its Daybreak Books imprint publishes books to help people understand their spiritual nature and learn how they can apply spirituality in everyday life. Direct queries to Neil Wertheimer, publisher.

St. Anthony Messenger Press

1615 Republic Street, Cincinnati, OH 45210

513-241-5615 • *www.americancatholic.org*

St. Anthony Messenger publishes books for readers who seek a richer Catholic, Christian, human life. It does not publish fiction, poetry, autobiography, personal reflections, academic studies, art, or coffee-table books, and it will not consider simultaneous submissions. Send a query letter and outline to Lisa Beidenbach, managing editor.

Saint Mary's Press

702 Terrace Heights, Winona, MN 55987-1320

507-457-7900 • *www.smp.org*

Saint Mary's Press is a Catholic house with a mission to provide a human and Christian education to young people. It will consider memoirs and is looking for character-driven young-adult novels of about

40,000 words that show the struggle toward adulthood. Direct queries to Steve Nagel, editor.

Simon & Schuster, Inc.

1230 Avenue of the Americas, New York, NY 10020

212-698-7000 • *www.simonsays.com*

Simon & Schuster's Fireside Books, in addition to its general non-fiction categories, emphasizes self-help, inspiration, New Age, and spirituality. Direct queries to Marcela Landres.

Sterling Publishing

387 Park Avenue South, New York, NY 10016

212-532-7160 • *www.sterlingpub.com*

Sterling publishes books whose spiritual and self-help topics are grounded in what is practical and helpful in our daily lives. Sterling is interested in books about subjects such as alternative health, ghosts, UFOs, Celtic topics, and healing. Query acquisitions editor Steve Magnuson.

Swedenborg Foundation Publishers

320 North Church Street, West Chester, PA 19380

610-430-3222, ext. 10 • *www.swedenborg.com*

The Swedenborg Foundation's Chrysalis Books publishes spiritual and personal-growth titles that have some connection, congruence, or reference to the theology of Emanuel Swedenborg (1688–1772). See the Web site for detailed submission guidelines. Chrysalis will accept unsolicited proposals.

Theosophical Publishing House

P.O. Box 270, Wheaton, IL 60189

630-665-0130 • *www.theosophical.org*

Theosophical Publishing House is a division of the Theosophical Society in America. Theosophy is the study of religion, philosophy, science, and one's search for union within the universe. Its imprint, Quest Books, prefers submissions from established authors but is most concerned that the writing is exceptional. Quest looks for spiritual self-help books. Its list includes books on Native American spirituality, women's and men's spirituality, Eastern and Western religions, and theosophy. Quest is not interested in personal spiritual-awakening stories. Send a query or proposal package to Brenda Rosen, acquisitions editor.

Time Warner Books

Time-Life Building, 1271 Avenue of the Americas, New York, NY 10020
212-522-7200 • *www.twbookmark.com*

While Time Warner does not accept unagented material, it encourages new writers to post material, at no charge, on Ipublish.com, where it can be considered for publication.

Tyndale House Publishers

P.O. Box 80, Wheaton, IL 60189 • 630-668-8310 • *www.tyndale.com*

Tyndale offers a well-rounded list of books on Christian living, devotional and inspirational topics, and general nonfiction from a nondenominational, biblically supportable perspective. This house also looks for religious fiction, especially mainstream novels and inspirational romance. It will consider evangelical Christian-theme novels that are set in a historical backdrop. See the Web site for submission information. Acquisitions editor is Ron Beers.

Union of American Hebrew Congregations Press

633 Third Avenue, New York, NY 10017
888-489-8242 • *www.uahc.org/press*

This house publishes high-quality religious, educational, and trade books from the Reform Jewish perspective. On the Web site is a "New Book Proposal" form that UAHC Press asks prospective authors to fill out. It can be either submitted electronically or printed out and faxed.

Zondervan

5300 Patterson Avenue Southeast, Grand Rapids, MI 49530

616-698-6900 • *www.zondervan.com*

Zondervan is a major publisher of evangelical Christian titles specializing in contemporary issues in spirituality and inspirational novels. Its mission is to bring positive and redemptive change into the lives of people worldwide. It looks to promote biblical principles and invests a great deal of effort in promoting and marketing its products. Zondervan prefers that unsolicited queries or proposals be submitted to "First Edition" on the Web site of the Evangelical Christian Publishers Association (*www.ecpa.org/FE/index.html*). Zondervan regularly reviews proposals posted to this site. There is a $79 posting fee per proposal.

Books, Organizations, Lists, Magazines, and Directories

American Book Trade Directory

Lists wholesalers and sales representatives for self-published books. Published by R. R. Bowker; available at most libraries.

The Association of Authors' Representatives, Inc.

P.O. Box 237201, Ansonia Station, New York, NY 10003

www.aar-online.org

For a list of member agents, send a request with an SASE (57 cents postage) and $7 to cover photocopying and handling to the address above, or check the list on-line.

The Christian Writer's Market Guide

By Sally E. Stuart. Writer's guidelines and submission procedures for all Christian publishing houses that accept unsolicited manuscripts.

The Directory of Publishers in Religion

Compiled by Mike Farry (Scholars Press Handbook Series).

Literary Market Place

Subtitled *The Directory of the American Book Publishing Industry with Industry Yellow Pages*. Lists U.S. and Canadian publishers, agents, printers, and editorial services, including contact and submission information as well as geographical indexes. U.S. publishers are categorized by types and subjects of books. Published annually by R. R. Bowker; available in the reference section at most libraries.

NAPRA ReView

Bimonthly trade magazine for retailers of body/mind/spirit books, gifts, media, and music. Published by the Networking Alternatives for Publishers, Retailers, and Artists, Inc.; see *www.napra.com*.

Publishers Directory

Lists contact information, number of new titles, editorial personnel, and subject interest of U.S. and Canadian publishers. Published annually by Gale Group; available in the reference section at libraries.

Publishers International ISBN Directory

Directory of periodical and book publishers, including small and alternative presses, institutions, and organizations. This is the most comprehensive source of publisher contact information, though it does not offer information on genres of material. Published by K. G. Saur.

Write the Perfect Book Proposal
By Jeff Herman and Deborah Adams (John Wiley & Sons, 1993).

Web Sites

Spiritual writers are truly blessed by the invention of the Internet. The World Wide Web provides writers the opportunity to explore every aspect of the publishing world: the industry, writing resources, connecting with other writers, and even finding sources of funding for certain types of projects. You may also explore the innumerable sites on spirituality and connect with like-minded people. Everything eventually connects to itself. So who knows? What first seems like something irrelevant could wind up bringing you to your destiny.

This annotated list of sites offers descriptions of some of the most useful sites for writers. For your convenience, sites are grouped in resource categories.

Media
Authors and Experts
www.authorsandexperts.com

A promotional database of "authors and experts" used by media members.

ENewsRelease.com
www.enewsrelease.com

A commercial news-distribution service.

Gebbie Press
www.gebbieinc.com

"The All-in-One Media Directory."

GuestFinder.com
www.guestfinder.com

"Where Great Interviews Begin." A media-contact service.

Media Finder
www.mediafinder.com

A comprehensive print-media database for the United States and Canada.

NetRead's EventCaster
www.netread.com/calendar

Broadcasts literary events to event editors at newspapers and Web sites.

Newspapers.com
www.newspapers.com

On-line catalog of national, local, and international papers.

PR Web
www.prweb.com

By PR professionals for PR professionals. A free press-release distribution service.

Radio Online
www.radioonline.com

"Radio's Starting Point in the Net." A comprehensive resource of radio information.

RadioSpace
www.radiospace.com

Radio-related current events, consumer information, and news.

Talion.com

www.talion.com

Offers a range of publicity programs, from small to large.

Talkers Magazine Online

www.talkers.com

"The Bible of Talk Radio," a trade publication serving the talk-radio industry.

TVTalkShows.com

www.tvtalkshows.com

A talk-show-fan Web site with news and gossip.

Writing and Publishing
1001 Ways to Market Your Books

www.bookmarket.com/1001bio.html

This site offers a book-marketing newsletter, consulting services, and book-marketing updates. Other topics include success letters, author bios, sample chapters, and tables of contents.

@writers: For Writers on the Internet

www.geocities.com/athens/6346/body.html

Includes information about markets, links to myriad Internet resources, reviews of writing-related books, and a technical Q&A section to answer questions about hardware, software, and the Internet. Also available is a chat room and monthly newsletter subscription.

American Booksellers Association

www.bookweb.org

The American Booksellers Association is a trade organization representing independent bookstores nationwide. The site links members to recent articles about the industry and features "Idea Exchange" discussion forums.

The Art Deadline

custwww.xensei.com/adl

This site offers a "monthly newsletter providing information about juried exhibitions and competitions, call for entries/proposals/papers, poetry and other writing contests, jobs, internships, scholarships, residencies, fellowships, casting calls, auditions, tryouts, grants, festivals, funding, financial aid, and other opportunities for artists, art educators, and art students of all ages. Some events take place on the Internet."

Association of American Publishers, Inc.

www.publishers.org/home/index.htm

The Association of American Publishers "is the principal trade association of the book publishing industry." The site includes information and registration for annual meetings and conferences, industry news, info about book publishing, industry stats and issues, and copyright data.

Association of Authors' Representatives, Inc.

www.bookwire.com/aar

The Association of Authors' Representatives, Inc., is "an organization of independent literary and dramatic agents." It is a member-only site that offers information about finding an agent, Internet links, a newsletter, and a canon of ethics.

Authorlink

www.authorlink.com

Doris Booth started Authorlink with people like you in mind. This is a great resource for writers as well as other industry professionals. She includes relevant writing articles and features a "Manuscript Showcase" with over 500 ready-to-publish manuscripts.

The Authors Guild

www.authorsguild.org

For more than eighty years the Guild has been the authoritative voice of American writers. Its strength is the foundation of the U.S. literary community. This site features sample contracts, and explanation of their terms, advice, a legal search, information on electronic rights, how to join the organization, a bulletin index, publishers row, a listing of board members, and current articles about the publishing field. There is also a link to *Back-in-print.com*, an online bookstore featuring out-of-print editions made available by their authors.

Aylad's Creative Writing Group

www.publication.com/aylad

This site provides a forum for "people to get their work read and critiqued by fellow writers in a friendly atmosphere." The service is free and all writing forms are welcome. The site includes links to other resources for writers.

Booklist

www.ala.org/booklist/index.html

This site is the digital counterpart of the American Library Association's *Booklist* magazine. In the site is a current selection of reviews, feature articles, and a searchable cumulative index. Review topics include books for youth, adult books, media, and reference materials. The site also includes press releases, the best-books list, and subscription information.

Booknote

www.booknote.com

Booknote specializes in custom-designed Web sites for authors, book titles, literary agents, and publishers. Their award-winning sites are individually designed to capture the creativity of the unique individuals they feature. They also extensively target-market each site to all relevant special-interest or news groups on the Web to increase both the person's recognition and Web sales.

Booknotes

www.booknotes.org/right.htm

Based on the book and television program *Booknotes*, aired on C-SPAN, this site allows one to learn about the authors who have appeared on the program, read transcripts from the program, watch RealVideo clips from authors who have been featured on the program, preview the upcoming *Booknotes* schedule, listen to recent *Booknotes* programs in RealAudio, and learn about the publishing industry in general. The site also features message boards and a link to the C-SPAN bookstore.

The Book Report

www.bookwire.com/tbr

The Book Report is "where readers meet readers and readers meet writers." It is a conversational site where visitors may talk about a book they have recently read or get tips on great new books from other visitors. The site also includes book reviews and transcriptions of exclusive chats with authors.

Bookreporter

www.bookreporter.com/brc/index.asp

Bookreporter offers book reviews and a perspectives section that deals with topics such as when a book becomes a movie. It features a daily quote by a famous author.

Booktalk

www.booktalk.com

This site is a publishing insider's page where you'll find out who's hot and what's up. It features links to get in touch with authors, agents, publishers, and bookstores, as well as a slush pile.

BookWire

www.bookwire.com

Partners with *Publishers Weekly*, *Literary Market Place*, and *Library Journal*, among others, BookWire is a site that offers book-industry news, reviews, original fiction, author interviews, and guides to literary events. The site features publicity and marketing opportunities for publishers, authors, booksellers, and publicists. It also includes a list of the latest BookWire press releases.

BookZone

www.bookzone.com

BookZone was created "to increase book sales and profits for publishers." This site offers information on writing, marketing, and business and legal issues for publishing professionals, as well as forums, publishing news, and on-line subscriptions to journals "at the guaranteed lowest prices on the Web." The site also features a "Super Catalog" of books, thousands of book-related links, as well as site hosting, development, and on-line marketing. "For design, development, e-commerce solutions, promotion and exposure, BookZone is the busiest and best Web host for publishers, authors, and other publishing professionals."

The Catholic Book Publishers Association

www.cbpa.org

Facilitates the sharing of professional information, networking, cooperation, and friendship among those involved in Catholic book publishing in the United States and abroad.

Coffeehouse for Writers

www.coffeehouse4writers.com

The Coffeehouse for Writers is an "online writer's colony; a place where writers—from novice to professional—gather to critique, advise, and encourage each other." The site provides links to other resources for writers and a list of suggested books.

Critique Partner Connections

www.petalsoflife.com/cpc.html

A user of Critique Partner Connections pays a one-time fee of $15 to be matched with a fellow writer for the purpose of critiquing one another's work. The site's producers strive to match people with similar interests and critique styles.

E-zine-list

www.meer.net/~johnl/e-zine-list

This list of electronic zines around the world is no longer being updated but is still helpful.

The Editorial Eye

www.eei-alex.com

This site consists of a sampler of articles originally printed in the newsletter of the same name. The articles discuss techniques for writing, editing, design, and typography, as well as information on industry trends and employment. *The Eye* has been providing information to publishing professionals for eighteen years.

The Editor's Pen
www.pathway.net/dwlcey/default.htm

This site exists to connect "sites for and about Writers, Editors, and Indexers." It includes links to lists of freelancers and on-line dictionaries. Other interesting links include an "Edit challenge" and "Quotable words of editorial wisdom."

Forwriters.com
www.forwriters.com

This "mega-site" provides numerous links to writing resources of all kinds. It lists conferences, markets, agents, commercial services, and more. The "What's New" feature allows the user to peruse what links have recently been added under the various categories.

Inkspot
www.inkspot.com

Inkspot provides articles, how-to tips, market information, and networking opportunities. Special features include FAQs for beginners, classifieds, and a section for young writers. Information is sorted by genre.

Inner Circle
www.geocities.com/soho/lofts/1498/circlefaq.htm

This site started in April 1997 as "a means for writers—especially new and unpublished writers—to correspond through e-mail with others of similar interest." Membership is free and provides the opportunity to communicate with over 1,500 writers from around the globe.

International Online Writers Association

www.project-iowa.org

IOWA's purpose is to "offer help and services to writers around the world through shared ideas, workshops, critiques, and professional advice." Services include real-time monthly workshops, real-time weekly critiques, and periodic round robins. The site also includes a library of essays, poems, short stories, and novel chapters.

Internet Writing Workshop

www.geocities.com/1kaus/workshop/index.html

This site exists to "create an environment where works in progress can be passed around and critiqued, to help us improve these works and to improve as writers," as well as to provide support for writers. The service is membership-based and includes a variety of genres.

Library Journal Digital

www.bookwire.com/ljdigital

Library Journal offers articles about news in the publishing industry, editorials, a calendar of events, video reviews, audiobook reviews, bestseller news, and a job-search section.

Literary Market Place

www.literarymarketplace.com/lmp/us/index_us.asp

LMP offers information about publishers, which are categorized by U.S. book publishers, Canadian book publishers, and independent presses, as well as literary agents, including illustration and lecture agents. The site also offers trade services and resources. Limited information is free; the full information found in the book is available to subscribers.

Local Writers Workshop

members.tripod.com/~lww_2/introduction.htm

This site is an Internet forum for works in progress, especially those "in the early stages of revision." The creators pride themselves on this membership-based site's community ethic.

Midwest Book Review

www.execpc.com/~mbr/bookwatch/mbr/pubinfo.html

Midwest Book Review produces *Bookwatch*, a weekly television program that reviews books, videos, music, CD-ROMs, and computer software, as well as five monthly newsletters for community and academic library systems, and much more. Founded in 1980.

Misc. Writing

www.scalar.com/mw

This is "a UseNet newsgroup that provides a forum for discussion of writing in all its forms—scholarly, technical, journalistic, and mere day-to-day communication." The Web site resources include a writer's bookstore and market information.

The National Writers Union

www.nwu.org

NWU is the trade union for freelance writers of all genres. The Web site provides links to various services of the union, including grievance resolution, insurance, job information, and databases.

Painted Rock

www.paintedrock.com/memvis/memvis1.htm

Painted Rock "provides services to nonpublished writers, published writers, and readers." Features on the site include information on a free twelve-week "Artist's Way" program, message boards, goal-writing groups, writing topics, a book-discussion group, a research listserv, and *The Rock*, an on-line magazine. In addition to its free services, the site offers paid on-line writing classes, a subscription-based newsletter, and two bookstores, as well as advertising, promotion for authors, and Web site hosting and design.

Para Publishing

www.parapublishing.com

Para Publishing offers "the industry's largest resources/publications guide," a customized book writing/publishing/promoting information kit, as well as current and back issues of their newsletter. The site also includes research links, a listing of suppliers, and mailing lists.

Pen American Center

www.pen.org

Pen is an international "membership organization of prominent literary writers and editors. As a major voice of the literary community, the organization seeks to defend the freedom of expression wherever it may be threatened, and to promote and encourage the recognition and reading of contemporary literature." The site links to information about several Pen-sponsored initiatives, including literary awards.

Publishers Weekly Online

publishersweekly.reviewsnews.com

Publishers Weekly offers news about the writing industry in general, as well as special features about reading and writing in general and genre writing. The site also includes news on children's books, bookselling, interviews, international book-industry news, and industry updates. If you want to know where the editors and agents get their information, you've found it. You can get into the minds of the industry and can develop ideas by looking at the trends. You will also learn about the business side of things.

Pure Fiction

www.purefiction.com/start.htm

This Web site is "for anyone who loves to read—or aspires to write—best-selling fiction." Based in London and New York, the site includes reviews, previews, writing advice, an on-line bookshop, a writers' showcase, Internet links, and more. It also has a mailing list.

Reference Shelf

alabanza.com/kabacoff/inter-links/reference.html

This site provides quick access to words, facts, and figures useful when writing and fact-checking. A special Words section features dictionaries, acronym finders, and links to computer-jargon. This is a great reference for the properly fastidious writer—which does not always define the "spiritual writer." This site can help our inner editor clean up the manuscript for presentation.

R. R. Bowker

www.bowker.com

This site offers a listing of books in print, books out of print, a directory of the book-publishing industry, a data-collection center for R. R. Bowker publications, and a directory of vendors to the publishing community. This is a good resource for researching the competition, but remember: If a book on your subject is out of print, you don't have to include it as competition when you make your submission.

Sensible Solutions for Getting Happily Published

www.happilypublished.com

This site is "designed to help writers, publishers, self-publishers, and everyone else who cares about reaching readers, including editors, agents, booksellers, reviewers, industry observers and talk show hosts . . . and aims to help books get into the hands of the people they were written for." It includes information about finding a publisher, ways for publishers to raise revenues, the self-publishing option, how to boost a book's sales, and sensible solutions for reaching readers.

SharpWriter.Com

www.sharpwriter.com

This is a practical resources page for writers of all types—a "writer's handy virtual desktop." Reference materials include style sheets, dictionaries, quotations, and job information. "The Office Peacemaker" offers to resolve grammar disputes in the workplace.

Shaw Guides, Inc., Writer's Conferences

www.shawguides.com

This is a subscription-based listing of sponsors and the following month's writers' conferences calendar. The site allows the user to search for information about four hundred conferences and workshops worldwide. An e-mail service can be used to get updates about conferences that meet user criteria for dates, topics, and locations. Other resources include "Quick Tips," links to organizations, and information about residencies and retreats. This comprehensive listing of conferences is invaluable because there are so many to choose from. Conferences are the best way to get out of writer's isolation and to meet people in the industry.

Small Publishers of North America

www.spannet.org/home.htm

This is the site for "independent presses, self-publishers, and savvy authors who realize if their books are to be successful, they must make them so." The site offers pages for "fun, facts, and financial gain." They also offer a newsletter.

United States Copyright Office

lcweb.loc.gov/copyright

The U.S. Copyright Office offers valuable information about copyright procedures and other basics. In addition, the user can download publications and forms as well as link to information about international copyright laws. But don't get too excited. A copyright is a nice thing to have, but unlike the rumors about Hollywood, there is little chance of someone stealing your manuscript idea. If your book is sold, the copyright work will be done by your publisher. If you want to get a jump on it, this site will simplify the procedure for you.

A Web of On-Line Dictionaries

www.geocities.com/westhollywood/castro/6101/dic/diction1.html

This index of on-line dictionaries includes 165 different languages and gives preference to free resources. A new feature allows the user to translate words from any European language to another.

The WELL (Whole Earth 'Lectronic Link)

www.well.com

Its creators call this on-line gathering place a "literate watering hole for thinkers from all walks of life."

Women Who Write

members.aol.com/jfavetti/womenww/www.html

A "collage of women based all over the United States with a passion for writing," the site provides useful links and a large dose of encouragement to women writers of all levels of experience.

WriteLinks

www.writelinks.com

This site provides an array of services, including workshops, personalized tutoring, and critique groups. "WriteLinks is designed to be of value to all writers, regardless of their experience, genre, or focus."

Write Page Author Listing Information
www.writepage.com/pageinfo.htm

This site offers authors a chance to create their own Web sites with the help of Callie Goble. It answers many of the questions that one might have about such an enterprise, such as "How long *can* my page be?" "How long does it take to get listed?" "What sort of exposure will my books get?" "What does the competition charge?" and much more.

The Writers' BBS: International Writers Community
www.writers-bbs.com/home.shtml

Intended for "authors, poets, journalists, and readers," the highlights of this site are its writers' chat rooms, discussion forums, and an e-zine for beginning writers called *Fish Eggs for the Soul*. The site also includes games, personal ads, copyright information, mailing lists, links, an adults-only section, and the on-line King James Bible.

Writersmarket.com
writersmarket.com/index_ns.asp

Comprehensive and up-to-date market-contact information as well as an encyclopedia of publishing terms.

Writers Net
www.writers.net

This site "helps build relationships between writers, publishers, editors, and literary agents." It consists of two main sections, "The Internet Directory of Published Writers," which includes a list of published works and a biographical statement for each writer, and "The Internet Directory of Literary Agents," which lists areas of specialization and a description of each agency. Both are searchable and include contact information. The site is a free service that hopes to "become an important, comprehensive matchmaking resource for writers, editors, publishers, and literary agents on the Internet."

Writers on the Net

www.writers.com

"Writers on the Net is a group of published writers and experienced writing teachers building an online community and resource for writers and aspiring writers." A subscription to the mailing list provides a description and schedule of classes provided by the site and a monthly newsletter.

Writerspace

www.writerspace.com

For those of us not born with silver microchips in our mouths, there couldn't be a better resource than this author-specific support for Web-building. Everybody's got a site, and we should capitalize on this opportunity for promotion. Web services are also provided for those who may already have Web sites but wish to include more interactivity in the way of bulletin boards, chat rooms, contests, and e-mail newsletters. The site also features an author spotlight, workshops, mailing lists, romance links, a guestbook, and information on adding your link.

The Writer's Retreat

www.angelfire.com/va/dmsforever/index.html

The objectives of this site are "to provide a meeting place for writers everywhere, to provide market information, to list relevant Internet links, to list inspirational and motivational information and quotations for writers of all races, creeds, and backgrounds, and to have and provide fun while doing it!"

Writer's Toolbox

www.geocities.com/athens/6346/body.html

The site contains a "diverse and ever-growing collection of Internet resources for writers." The resources are categorized for many types of writers, from technical writers and PR professionals to fiction and drama writers. The site also includes links to software for writers and business resources.

Writers Write

www.writerswrite.com

This mega-site provides myriad resources, including a searchable database of on-line and print publications in need of submissions. The chat room is open twenty-four hours for live discussion.

YouCanWrite.com

youcanwrite.com

"The Online Reality Check for Aspiring Writers of Nonfiction Books" is a 2001 Winner of the *Writer's Digest* 101 Best Web Sites for Writers.

Poetry

Here are some sites that may prove useful to the aspiring spiritual poet.

Atlantic Unbound Poetry Pages

www.theatlantic.com/atlantic/atlweb/poetry/poetpage.htm

Brought to you by *Atlantic Monthly*, a literary magazine, this site offers reviews of new poetry, a discussion forum, and the "Audible Anthology," which is a collection of poetry sound files, poetry articles, links, and poetry from the *Atlantic Monthly* on-line zine. It is a searchable site and offers poetry and literature links.

Electronic Poetry Center

wings.buffalo.edu/epc

There are perhaps more poetry sites on-line than any other literary genre, so picking one representative site is really quite difficult. But we do recommend this one, based out of the University of New York at Buffalo. They are at the heart of the contemporary poetry community on-line, having been around since the early days of gopher space, practically the Dark Ages in computer time. Of particular note is the active and well-respected poetics mailing list, the large collection of audio files, and an extensive listing of small-press poetry publishers.

Inkspot Resources for Poets

www.inkspot.com/ss/genres/poetry.html

This site offers poetry links, a poets' chat forum, contests, general resources (such as a glossary of poetic terms), mailing lists, courses available, critique groups and workshops for poets, and articles and essays on writing poetry.

The International Library of Poetry

www.poetry.com

The ILP offers information about its writing competitions, which focus on "awarding large prizes to poets who have never before won any type of writing competition." The site also includes links, a list of past winners, anthologies of winning poems, and chat rooms.

National Poetry Association

www.nationalpoetry.org

Supported in part by Grants for the Arts and Maya Angelou, this site offers an on-line poetry journal called *Poetry USA* and aims to "promote poets and poetry to wider audiences by all possible means, serving both the literary community and the general public." The site is dedicated to the memory of William Burroughs, Allen Ginsberg, Denise Levertov, and Jack Micheline. It includes information about the NPA's current projects and offers contests for poets.

Poetry from the Mining Co.

poetry.miningco.com

This site offers links to such poetry resources as on-line contests and workshops, zines, anthologies, poets from the classical period to the twentieth century, multilingual and poetry translations, festivals and live poetry events, audio poetry archives, publishers, and on-line catalogs. It also includes a poetry newsletter, bulletin board, chat room, bookstore, and gossip, as well as "an alphabetical listing and links to online lit zines, anthologies, and the online sites of print poetry magazines."

Poetry Society of America

www.poetrysociety.org

Includes information about the newest developments in the Poetry in Motion project, which posts poetry to seven million subway and bus riders in New York City, Chicago, Baltimore, Portland (Oregon), and Boston. It also includes news about poetry awards, seminars, the tributes in libraries program, poetry in public program, and poetry festivals.

Poets & Writers

www.pw.org

This on-line resource for creative writers includes publishing advice, message forums, contests, a directory of writers, literary links, information on grants and awards, news from the writing world, trivia, and workshops.

Children's Books

There is a small but solid market for spiritual work for children and young adults. Here's a sample of on-line resources. Many aren't geared specifically to spiritual material. For houses that handle spiritual children's books, refer to the listing of publishers.

The Children's Book Council
www.cbcbooks.org

"CBC Online is the Web site of the Children's Book Council—encouraging reading since 1945." It provides a list of articles geared toward publishers, teachers, librarians, booksellers, parents, authors, and illustrators—all those who are interested in the children's book field.

Children's Writing Resource Center
www.write4kids.com

"Whether you're published, a beginner, or just someone who's always dreamt of writing for kids," here you'll find a free library of how-to information, opportunities to chat with other children's writers and illustrators, links to research databases, articles, tips for beginners, secrets for success as a children's writer, message boards, a children's writing survey, the chance to ask questions of known authors, and the opportunity to register in the guestbook to receive free e-mail updates filled with news and tips. The site also features a listing of favorite books, Newbery and Caldecott Medal winners, current best-sellers, and a link to its own children's bookshop.

The Society of Children's Book Writers and Illustrators
www.scbwi.org

This Web site "has a dual purpose: It exists as a service to our members, as well as offering information about the children's publishing industry and our organization to nonmembers." It features a listing of events, awards and grants, publications, information for members, information on how to become a member, and a site map.

Spiritual Web Sites and Magazines

This list is intended to give you a sense of the range of subjects covered by spiritual magazines, though it is impossible to be truly representative. It would take several lifetimes to exhaust the list of these sites, especially since new ones are added every day. No matter how obscure your interest, you will find that there are always people who share it. Magazines can offer spiritual writers freelance opportunities to build up a portfolio of clippings. If you are published in your book's subject, such articles improve your credibility. Note that while freelancing can give many intangible rewards that make it worth pursuing, you won't get rich from it.

Adventist Today

www.atoday.com/magazine

A bimonthly magazine reporting on contemporary issues of importance to Adventist church members plus breaking news. Archive of past issues and opportunities for interaction/discussion.

Amen Christian Magazine

www.raleighcommunity.org/amen

A multimedia e-zine designed to present the gospel over the Internet.

Awareness Magazine

www.awarenessmag.com

A bimonthly publication that reaches individuals concerned with many issues that involve the environment, holistic health, natural health products, fitness, and personal growth.

Bodhi Tree Bookstore

www.bodhitree.com

This site offers books, recorded material, spiritual accessories, and gifts.

Body and Soul

www.newage.com

Formerly *New Age Journal*, this magazine has a mission to inspire and empower people in their quest for a healthier and more spiritually fulfilling life.

The Catholic Book Publishers Association

www.cbpa.org

Despite the name, it's not just for Roman Catholic publishers. This site has a great list of publishers with both contact information and the types of books published. The site facilitates the sharing of professional information, networking, cooperation, and friendship among those involved in Catholic book publishing in the United States and abroad.

East West Books

www.eastwest.com

The deepest line of New Age and spiritual books on the Net.

Focus Magazine

www.focusmagazine.org

Christianity Magazine recently combined forces with *Focus Magazine*.

Freeware Esoteric to Spiritual

www.moonxscape.com/freeware.htm

Programs to download on such diverse topics as astrology, Feng Shui, tao, runes, and biorhythms, as well as religious and spiritual texts.

Hinduism Today

www.hinduismtoday.com

A news magazine articulating Indian spirituality.

Inner Star Magazine

www.newage.com.au/home/inner-star.html

Covers topics such as tarot, angels, meditation, spiritual development, healing, reincarnation, auras, dreams, crystals, and numerology.

Jewish Family and Life

www.jewishfamily.com

Reflects the strong family traditions of Jewish culture in modern language. Includes information on travel, health, food, and more.

Magical Blend

www.magicalblend.com

An alternative spirituality magazine dedicated to improving lives.

MindBodySpirit Internet Magazine

www.mindbodyspirit.com.au/magazine.htm

A directory-type e-zine with links to a wide variety of New Age articles on mainly Australian sites.

New Leaf Distributing

www.newleaf-dist.com

A large distributor of books and other informational materials that
foster learning, personal awakening, spiritual growth, and healing.

Organic Style

www.organicstyle.com

This magazine from Rodale focuses on the art of living in balance.

Oracle

www.appleonline.net/oracle/default.htm

A British magazine with a fresh outlook on spiritual matters. Includes article samples, subscription information, and more.

PanGaia

www.pangaia.com

A well-respected magazine for pagans, Gaians, and Wiccans. It buys first- and third-person nonfiction, poetry, and fiction.

Parabola: Myth, Tradition, and the Search for Meaning

www.parabola.org

A magazine published by members of the Gurdjieff Foundation about the study of the myths, rituals, symbols, and arts of the world's spiritual traditions.

Precious Seed Magazine

www.preciousseed.org

A magazine to encourage study of the Scriptures, practice of New Testament church principles, and interest in gospel work.

Religions & Spiritualities Chat Transcripts

www.talkcity.com/religions/transcript.html

Talk City chats with authors and experts.

Response

gbgm-umc.org/response

The voice of women in mission and a magazine for all Christians who want to be a part of a more peaceful, just world where all people are children of God.

Ruminator Review

www.ruminator.com

A theme-based quarterly book magazine featuring essays, interviews, and in-depth reviews.

SageWoman

www.sagewoman.com

The largest-circulation magazine for goddess-oriented women. It buys first-person women's narratives on specific themes.

Shambhala Sun Online

www.shambhalasun.com

A Buddhist magazine that applies the wisdom of the world's great contemplative traditions to the arts, social issues, politics, and health.

Spiritual Sisters of the Internet Cafe

www.spiritualsisters.com

A place of spiritual rest, inspiration, and support.

Songs of Deliverance Magazine

www.angelfire.com/ok/cindydavis

An on-line Christian magazine that helps promote spiritual growth for those seeking a deeper walk with God.

Transitions Bookplace

transitionsbookplace.com

These spiritual bookstore innovators have a variety of interesting events including a newsletter, Buddhist reading group, and book club.

Wisdom Magazine

www.wisdom-magazine.com

Monthly publication dealing with the philosophies, services, and products of the New Age lifestyle.

Women of Spirit

www.womenofspirit.com

An Adventist bimonthly magazine that allows readers to see how other women are dealing with issues like health, divorce, childrearing, spiritual life, friendship, and single life. Includes an archive of past stories, staff interviews, subscribing information, and links to women's resources.

YouthNews Magazine Online

youthnews.faithweb.com

Music, poems, articles, games, events, art, real-life stories, prayer, and support for the brokenhearted—all through the eyes of young Christian people.

EPILOGUE

As you now spread your wings and begin your journey toward publication, do not forget why you began. You are called to write because there is a higher calling that you must satisfy. If you try to ignore it, you will be forever filled with a sense of something yet undone. It will haunt you. Whether or not anyone ever reads what you write, you need your gift of writing to learn your own truth. So try not to allow the race toward publication to cloud the process that is so enriching for you and for those who can bask in the glow of your inner light.

There is so much to do! You have an important role in the process of our collective awakening to higher truth. Writers have influence. Good writers—those who allow their message to outweigh their need for personal recognition—can change the world. Take pride in your work and glory in your achievements, but don't forget that all spiritual writing comes from the same source. You are a collaborator who we pray will remember to thank your co-creator.

May the creative force of the universe light your way to the fulfillment of your chosen destiny. And may you never forget your SASE!

GLOSSARY

advance. Money paid (usually in installments) to an author by a publisher prior to publication. The advance is paid against royalties; if an author is given a $5,000 advance, for instance, the author will collect royalties only after the royalty moneys due exceed $5,000. A good contract protects the advance if it should exceed the royalties ultimately due from sales.

advance orders. Orders received any time before a book's official publication date.

agent. The person who acts on behalf of the author to handle the sale and negotiations of the author's work. Agents are paid on a percentage basis from the money owed to their author clients.

American Booksellers Association (ABA). The major trade organization for chain and independent retail booksellers. During BookExpo America, the annual ABA convention and trade show, publishers and distributors can display their wares to the industry at large. It also provides a networking forum for booksellers, editors, agents, publicists, and authors.

auction. The event that takes place when an agent believes a manuscript to be a hot property (such as a possible best-seller with strong subsidiary-rights potential). The agent offers the work to multiple publishing houses for confidential bidding. Likewise, other rights such as reprint and film may be auctioned off by a successful book's original publisher's subsidiary-rights department or by the author's agent.

audio books. Spoken-word adaptations of works originally created and produced in print. These works are produced for distribution on audio media, typically audiotape cassette or audio compact disc (CD). Sometimes they feature the author's own voice; many are given dramatic readings by one or more actors, at times embellished with sound effects.

author's copies/author's discount. Author's copies are the free copies of the book that the author receives from the publisher; the exact number is negotiated before the contract is signed—usually at least ten. The author's discount allows the author to purchase additional copies (usually at a 40 percent discount from the retail price) and resell them at readings, lectures, and other public engagements.

author tour. A series of appearances by an author to promote and publicize his or her book.

backlist. Titles published prior to the current season and still in print. Such books often represent the publisher's cash-flow mainstays. Although many backlist titles may be difficult to find in bookstores, they can be ordered through a local bookseller or directly from the publisher. *Compare* **frontlist.**

back matter. Elements of a book that follow the text. Back matter may include the appendix, notes, glossary, bibliography, resources, index, author biography, list of additional books from the author and publisher, and colophon.

best-seller. Those titles that move in the largest quantities, based on sales or orders by bookstores, wholesalers, and distributors. Lists of best-sellers can be local (as in metropolitan newspapers), regional (as in geographically keyed trade or consumer periodicals), or national (as in *USA Today, Publishers Weekly,* or the *New York Times*), as well as international. Fiction and nonfiction are usually listed separately, as are hardcover and paperback.

bibliography. A list of books, articles, and other sources used in the research and writing of the book's text.

blues *or* **bluelines.** Proofs of the printing plates for a book, reviewed as a means to inspect the set type and layout for errors before the book goes to press.

blurb. Written copy or an extracted quotation used for publicity and promotional purposes, as on a flyer, in a catalog, or in an advertisement. *See* **cover blurbs**.

book club. A book-marketing operation that ships selected titles to subscribing members on a regular basis, sometimes at greatly reduced prices. Sales to book clubs are negotiated through the publisher's subsidiary-rights department. (In the case of a best-seller or other work that has gained acclaim, these rights can be auctioned off.) Terms vary, but the split of royalties between author and publisher is often 50-50.

book producer *or* **book packager.** Someone who conceives an idea for a book (most often nonfiction) or series, brings together the professionals (including the writer) needed to produce the book(s), sells the project to a publisher, and takes the project through to manufactured product—or performs any selection of those functions, as commissioned by the publisher or other client. The book producer may negotiate separate contracts with the publisher and with the writers, editors, and illustrators who contribute to the book.

book review. A critical appraisal of a book that evaluates such aspects as organization and writing style, possible market appeal, and cultural, political, or literary significance. A positive review from a respected book-trade journal such as *Publishers Weekly, Kirkus Reviews, Library Journal,* or *Booklist* will encourage booksellers to order the book. Copies of these raves will be used for promotion and publicity purposes by the publisher and will encourage reviewers nationwide to review the book.

Books in Print. Listings, published by R. R. Bowker, of books currently in print. These yearly volumes (along with periodic supplements such as *Forthcoming Books in Print*) provide ordering information including title, author, ISBN, price, publisher, and whether the book is available in hardcover or paperback or with library binding.

Listings are provided alphabetically by author, title, and subject area. Can be found in libraries and some bookstores.

bound galleys. Copies of uncorrected typesetter's page proofs or printouts of electronically produced mechanicals that are bound together to distribute to potential reviewers before a book's publication. *Compare* **galleys**. Bound galleys are sent to trade journals as well as to a limited number of reviewers who require long lead times.

bulk sales. The sale at a set discount of many copies of a single title—the greater the number of books, the larger the discount.

byline. The name of the author of a given piece, identifying him or her as the author of a book or article. Ghostwriters, by definition, do not receive bylines.

Christian. A category of books and writing in which Christian theology, dogma, and strictures is integral, not incidental, to the core message.

co-author. One who shares authorship of a work. Co-authors have bylines and share royalties based on their contributions to the book. *Compare* **ghostwriter**.

collaboration. A term denoting the working relationship that occurs when a writer wishes to work with another person in order to produce books outside the writer's own area of expertise. (For example, a writer with an interest in antiques may collaborate with a historian to increase the scope of a book.) The writer may be billed as a *co-author* or as *ghostwriter*. Royalties are shared, based on respective contributions to the book, including expertise, promotional abilities, and actual writing of the book.

colophon. A publisher's logo, although the term also applies to a listing of the fonts and materials used in the book production and credits for the design, composition, and production of the book. Such colophons are usually included in the back matter or as part of the copyright page.

commercial books. Books that appeal to a broad, nonacademic audience.

concept. A general statement of the idea behind a book.

contract. A legally binding document between author and publisher that sets the terms for the advance, royalties, subsidiary rights, advertising, promotion, publicity, and many other contingencies and responsibilities.

cooperative advertising, *or* **co-op.** An advertising agreement between a publisher and a bookstore. The publisher's book is featured in an ad for the bookstore (often in conjunction with an author appearance), and the publisher contributes to the cost of the ad.

copy editor. An editor responsible for the final polishing of a manuscript, who reads primarily in terms of appropriate word usage and grammar, with an eye toward clarity and coherence, factual errors and inconsistencies, spelling, and punctuation. Also called *line editor*. *See also* **editor.**

copyright. The legal proprietary right to reproduce, publish, and sell copies of literary, musical, and other artistic works. The rights to literary properties reside in the author from the time the work is produced, regardless of whether or not a formal copyright registration is obtained. However, for legal recourse in the event of plagiarism or other infringement, the work must be registered with the U.S. Copyright Office, and all copies of the work must bear the copyright notice. *See also* **work-for-hire.**

cover blurbs. Endorsing quotes from other writers, celebrities, or experts in a book's subject area. On the cover or dust jacket, they enhance the book's point-of-purchase appeal.

deadline. The author's due date for delivery of the completed manuscript to the publisher. It can be as much as a full year before official publication date.

delivery. Submission of the completed manuscript to the editor or publisher.

direct marketing. Advertising that involves a "direct response" (which is an equivalent term) from a consumer—for instance, order forms, coupons, or mailings directed at buyers presumed to hold a special interest in a particular book.

display titles. Books designed to be eye-catching to the casual shopper in a bookstore setting often with the intention of piquing book-buyer excitement about the store's stock in general. Many display titles with attractive cover art are stacked on their own freestanding racks; sometimes broad tables are laden with these items. A book shelved with its front cover showing on racks along with diverse other titles is technically a display title. Promotional or premium titles are likely to be display items, as are mass-market paperbacks and hardbacks with best-seller potential.

distribution. The method of getting books from the production stage into the reader's hands. Distribution is traditionally through bookstores, but it can also include such means as telemarketing and mail-order sales, special-interest outlets such as health-food or New Age venues, sports and fitness emporiums, or gift shops. Publishers use their own sales forces as well as independent salespeople, wholesalers, and distributors. Many large and some small publishers distribute for other publishers.

distributor. An agent or business that buys books from a publisher to resell, at a higher cost, to wholesalers, retailers, or individuals. Distribution houses are often excellent marketing enterprises because of their sales representatives, publicity and promotion personnel, and house catalogs. Skillful use of distribution networks can give a small publisher considerable national visibility.

dust jacket. The wrapper that covers hardcover books, designed by the publisher's art department or a freelance artist. Dust jackets were originally conceived to protect the book during shipping, but now their function is primarily to entice the browser with graphics and promotional copy to actually pick up the book.

dust-jacket copy. Descriptive text printed on the dust-jacket flaps that is written by the book's editor, in-house copywriters, or freelance specialists. Quotable praise the author has received from other writers, experts, and celebrities often appears on the jacket. *See also* **blurb.**

editor. Editorial responsibilities and titles vary from house to house, often being less strictly defined in smaller houses. The duties of the editor in chief or executive editor are primarily administrative: managing personnel, scheduling, budgeting, and defining the editorial personality of the firm or imprint. Senior editors and acquisitions editors acquire manuscripts (and authors), conceive project ideas and find writers to carry them out, and may oversee the writing and rewriting of manuscripts. Managing editors coordinate and schedule the book through the various phases of production. Associate and assistant editors are involved in much of the rewriting and reshaping of the manuscript and may also have acquisitions duties. Copy editors style the manuscript for punctuation, grammar, spelling, headings and subheadings, and so forth. Editorial assistants, in addition to general office work, perform some editorial duties as well—often as springboards to senior editorial positions.

endnotes. Explanatory notes and source citations that appear either at the end of individual chapters or at the end of a book's text, usually in scholarly works. *Compare* **footnotes.**

epilogue. The final segment of a book that offers commentary or further information but does not bear directly on the book's central design.

footnotes. Explanatory notes and source citations that appear at the bottom of a page. Footnotes are rare in general-interest books; instead such information is contained in endnotes or worked into the text or listed in the bibliography.

foreign agents. People who work with their U.S. counterparts to acquire rights for books from the United States for publication abroad. They can also represent U.S. publishers directly.

foreign market. Any foreign entity, such as a publisher or broadcast medium, that buys rights. Authors either share royalties with whoever negotiates the deal or keep 100 percent if they do their own negotiating.

foreign rights. Translation or reprint rights that can be sold to other countries. Foreign rights belong to the author but can be sold either country-by-country or as world rights. Often the U.S. publisher will own world rights, and the author will be entitled to anywhere from 50 to 85 percent of these revenues.

foreword. An introductory piece usually written by someone other than the author, such as an expert in the given field. If written by a celebrity or well-respected authority, the foreword can be a strong selling point for a prospective author and the book itself. *Contrast* **introduction.**

Frankfurt Book Fair. The largest international publishing exhibition, with a five-hundred-year history. This annual event in Frankfurt, Germany, provides an opportunity for thousands of publishers, agents, and writers from all over the world to negotiate, network, and buy and sell rights.

freight passthrough. The bookseller's freight cost (the cost of getting the book from the publisher to the bookseller). It is added to the basic invoice price the publisher charges the bookseller.

frontlist. New titles published in a given season by a publisher. Frontlist titles usually receive priority exposure in the front of the sales catalog—as opposed to backlist titles, which are usually found at the back of the catalog. *Compare* **backlist.**

front matter. The elements that precede the text of the work, including the title page, copyright page, dedication, table of contents, foreword, preface, acknowledgments, and introduction.

fulfillment house. A firm commissioned to fulfill orders for a publisher. Services may include warehousing, shipping, receiving returns, and mail-order and direct-marketing functions. Although more common for magazine publishers, fulfillment houses also serve book publishers.

galleys *or* **galley proofs.** Printouts from the typesetter of the electronically produced setup of the book's interior—the author's last chance to check for typos and make (usually minimal) revisions or additions to the copy. *See also* **bound galleys.**

ghostwriter. A writer without a byline, often without the remuneration and recognition that credited authors receive. Ghostwriters often get flat fees for their work instead of royalties. *Compare* **co-author.**

hardcover. Books bound in a format that conventionally includes thick, sturdy binding, a cover made usually of cloth spine and finished binding paper, and a dust jacket for a wrapper. *See also* **dust jacket.**

hook. A term denoting the distinctive concept or theme of a work that sets it apart as being fresh, new, or different from others in its field. A hook can be an author's special point of view, often encapsulated in a catchy or provocative phrase intended to attract or pique the interest of a reader, editor, or agent and turn the work into an exciting, commercially attractive package.

imprint. A separate line of product within a publishing house. Houses can have imprints composed of one or two series to those offering full-fledged and diversified lists. Imprints vary in their autonomy from the parent company. An imprint may have its own editorial department (perhaps consisting of just one editor), or house acquisitions editors may assign particular titles for release on appropriate specialized imprints. An individual imprint's categories often overlap with other imprints or with the publisher's core list, but some imprints maintain a small-house feel within an otherwise enormous conglomerate. The imprint can offer the distinct advantages of a personalized editorial approach while availing itself of the larger company's production, publicity, marketing, sales, and advertising resources.

index. An alphabetical directory at the end of a book that references names and subjects discussed in the book and the pages where such mentions can be found.

inspirational. A category of books characterized by their inspiring and uplifting content, often containing stories of triumph over tragedy, frequently given as gifts.

introduction. Preliminary remarks pertaining to a book. An introduction can be written by the author or an appropriate authority on the subject. If a book has both a foreword and an introduction, the foreword will be written by someone other than the author; the introduction will be written by the book's author and will be more closely tied to the text. *Contrast* **foreword.**

ISBN (International Standard Book Number). A ten-digit number that identifies the title and publisher of a book. It is used for ordering and cataloging the book and appears on the dust jacket, the back cover, and the copyright page.

ISSN (International Standard Serial Number). An eight-digit cataloging and ordering number that identifies all U.S. and foreign periodicals.

Library of Congress. The largest library in the world, located in Washington, D.C. The LOC can supply a writer with up-to-date sources and bibliographies in all fields, from arts and humanities to science and technology. For more information, write to the Library of Congress, Central Services Division, Washington, DC 20540.

Library of Congress Catalog Card Number. An identifying number issued by the Library of Congress to books it has accepted for its collection. The publication of those books, which are submitted by the publisher, are announced by the Library of Congress to libraries, which use Library of Congress numbers for their own ordering and cataloging purposes.

list. A publishing house's collection of books published, further refined as the *frontlist* and *backlist* to distinguish new titles from older ones.

Literary Market Place (LMP). An annual directory of the publishing industry that contains a comprehensive list of publishers with their addresses, phone numbers, some personnel, and the types of books they publish. Other listings include literary agencies, writers' conferences and competitions, and editorial and distribution services. *LMP* is published by R. R. Bowker and is available in most public libraries.

marketing plan. The strategy for selling a book, including its publicity, promotion, sales, and advertising.

mass-market paperback. Less-expensive smaller-format paperbacks sold from racks in supermarkets, variety stores, drugstores, and specialty shops as well as in bookstores. Also called *rack* (or *rack-sized*) editions. *Compare* **trade books**.

midlist. Books that traditionally form the bulk of a large publisher's list—nowadays often by default rather than intent. Midlist books are expected to be commercially viable but not explosive bestsellers. Agents may view such projects as a poor return for the effort, since they generally garner a low-end advance; to editors and publishers (especially the sales force), they are often difficult to market; prospective readers often find midlist books hard to buy in bookstores, as they have short shelf lives.

multiple contract. A book contract that includes a provisional agreement for a future book or books. *See also* **option clause**.

multiple submission. The submission of the same material to more than one publisher at once. Although multiple submission is a common practice, publishers should always be made aware that it is being done. Multiple submission by an author to several agents, on the other hand, is not as widely accepted. Also called *simultaneous submission*.

net receipts. The amount of money a publisher actually receives for sales of a book: the retail price minus the bookseller's discount or other discount. Once the cost of distribution and the number of returned copies is factored in, the net amount received per book is even lower. Royalties are usually figured on these net amounts rather than on the retail price of the book.

New Age. A category of books covering transformation, meditation, channeling, pyramids, ancient mysticism, shamanism, Native American spirituality, crystals, alternative health, energy work, and spiritualism.

occult. Having to do with esoteric, mysterious, or supernatural spiritual practices such as tarot cards, divination, Wicca, psychic phenomena, mediumship, astrology, dousing, or astral projection.

option clause. A clause in a book contract which stipulates that the publisher will have the exclusive right to consider and make an offer for the author's next book. However, the publisher is under no obligation to publish the book, and in most variations of the clause the author may opt for publication elsewhere. Also called *right of first refusal*. *See also* **multiple contract**.

outline. A hierarchical listing of a book's topics that provides the writer (and the proposal reader) with an overview of the ideas in a book in the order in which they are to be presented. *Compare* **synopsis**.

out-of-print books. Books no longer available from the publisher; rights usually revert to the author. *See also* **out of stock indefinitely**.

out of stock indefinitely. Another term for out-of-print books intended to soften the finality of the more common term. *See also* **out-of-print books**.

package. The book itself.

packager. *See* **book producer**.

page proof. The final typeset copy of the book, in page-layout form, before it is sent to the printer. *See also* **galleys**.

paperback. Books bound with a flexible, stress-resistant, paper covering.

permissions. The right to quote or reprint previously published material, obtained by the author early in the publishing process from the copyright holder.

plagiarism. The false presentation of someone else's writing as one's own. In the case of copyrighted work, plagiarism is illegal.

preface. An element of a book's front matter. In it, the author may discuss the purpose behind the format of the book, the type of research upon which it is based, its genesis, or its underlying philosophy.

premium. Books sold at a reduced price as part of a special promotion. Premiums can be sold to a bookseller, who in turn sells them to the book buyer (as with a line of modestly priced art books). Alternatively, such books may be produced as part of a broader marketing package. For instance, an organization may acquire a number of books for use in personnel training and as giveaways to clients. *See also* **special sales**.

press kit. A promotional package that includes a book's press release, author biography and photograph, reviews, and other pertinent information. The press kit can be created by the publisher's publicity department or an independent publicist and sent with a review copy of the book to potential reviewers and to media professionals who book author appearances.

price. There are two prices for a book: the amount the publisher charges the bookseller is the invoice price; the amount the consumer pays is the retail, cover, or list price.

proposal. A detailed presentation of the book's concept that includes such elements as a marketing plan, the author's credentials, and an analysis of competitive titles. It is used to gain the interest and services of an agent and to sell the project to a publisher.

publication date *or* pub date. A book's official date of publication, customarily set by the publisher to fall four to six weeks after completed bound books are delivered from the printer. The publication date is used to plan the title's promotional activities so that books will have had adequate time to arrive in stores to coincide with the appearance of advertising and publicity.

publicist. The publicity professional who handles press releases for new books and arranges the author's publicity tours, interviews, speaking engagements, and book-signings.

publisher's catalog. A seasonal sales catalog that lists and describes a publisher's new books and backlist titles. It is usually sent to potential buyers. Catalogs range from the basic to the glitzy and often include information on the authors, on print quantities, and on the publicity and promotion budget.

publisher's discount. The percentage by which a publisher discounts the retail price of a book to a bookseller, often partially based on the number of copies purchased.

Publishers' Trade List Annual. A collection of current and backlist catalogs arranged alphabetically by publisher, available in many libraries.

Publishers Weekly (PW). The publishing industry's chief trade journal. *PW* carries announcements of upcoming books, respected book reviews, interviews with authors and publishing-industry professionals, special reports on various book categories, and trade news (such as mergers, rights sales, and personnel changes).

query letter. A brief written presentation to an agent or editor designed to pitch both the author and the book idea.

religious. A category of books characterized by research-heavy text about major world religions.

remainders. Unsold book stock purchased from the publisher at a large discount and resold to the public.

reprint. A subsequent edition of a book already in print, especially publication in a different format (for example, the paperback reprint of a hardcover).

returns. Unsold books a bookstore returns to a publisher, for which the store may receive full or partial credit (depending on the publisher's policy, the age of the book, and other factors).

reversion-of-rights clause. A clause in the book contract which states that if the book goes out of print or the publisher fails to reprint the book within a stipulated length of time, all rights revert to the author.

review copy. A free copy of a book that the publisher sends to print and electronic media which review books for their audiences.

royalty. The percentage of the retail cost of a book that is paid to the author for each copy sold after the author's advance has been recouped. Some publishers structure royalties as a percentage payment against net receipts.

sales conference. A meeting of a publisher's editorial, sales, promotion, and publicity departments that covers the upcoming season's new books and marketing strategies for each.

sales representative *or* **sales rep.** A member of the publisher's sales force or an independent contractor who sells books to retailers in a certain territory.

SASE (self-addressed, stamped envelope). An essential element for an author to include with query letters, proposals, and manuscript submissions. Many editors and agents do not reply if a writer has neglected to enclose an SASE or has failed to provide the correct amount of postage.

satisfactory clause. A clause in the book contract that enables the publisher to refuse publication of a manuscript which is not deemed satisfactory. The specific criteria for publisher satisfaction should be set forth in the contract to protect the author from being forced to pay back the publisher's advance should the work be deemed unsatisfactory.

season. The time period in which publishers introduce their new line of books. Most publishers announce books for the spring and fall seasons.

self-publishing. A publishing project wherein an author pays for the costs of manufacturing and selling his or her own book and retains all money from the book's sale. This is a risky venture but one that can be highly profitable when combined with speaking engagements or imaginative marketing techniques; if successful, self-publication can lead to distribution or publication by a commercial publisher. *Compare* **subsidy publishing**.

serial rights. Reprint rights sold to periodicals. First serial rights include the right to publish the material before any other publication (generally before the book is released, or coinciding with the book's pub date). Second serial rights cover material already published, either in a book or another periodical.

series. Books published as a group either because of their related subject matter or authorship.

shelf life. The length of time a book remains on the bookstore shelf before it is pulled to make room for newer incoming stock.

signature. A group of book pages printed together on one large sheet of paper that is then folded and cut in preparation for being bound, along with the book's other signatures, into the final product.

simultaneous publication. The simultaneous issuing of more than one edition of a work, such as in hardcover and trade paperback. Simultaneous releases can be expanded to include gift editions as well as mass-market paper versions. Audio versions of books most often coincide with the release of the first print edition.

simultaneous submission. *See* **multiple submission**.

slush pile. Unsolicited manuscripts at a publishing house or literary agency awaiting review. Some publishers or agencies do not maintain slush piles per se but instead return unsolicited manuscripts without review (if an SASE is included). Querying a targeted publisher or agent before submitting a manuscript is an excellent way of avoiding the slush pile.

special sales. Sales of a book to appropriate retailers other than bookstores (for example, wine guides to liquor stores). This classification also includes books sold as premiums (*see* **premiums**) or for other promotional purposes. Depending on volume, per-unit costs can be very low, and the book can be custom-designed.

subsidiary rights. The reprint, serial, movie and television, and audiotape and videotape rights deriving from a book. The publisher and author negotiate the division of profits from the sales of these rights.

subsidy publishing. A mode of publication wherein the author pays a publishing company to produce his or her work, which may thus appear superficially to have been published conventionally. Also known as vanity publishing, subsidy publishing is generally more expensive than self-publishing because subsidy houses make a profit on all their contracted functions, charging fees well beyond the publisher's basic costs for production and services. *See also* **vanity press.**

synopsis. A book summary in paragraph form, rather than in outline format, that serves as an important part of a book proposal. For fiction, the synopsis succinctly and dramatically describes the highlights of story line and plot. For nonfiction, the synopsis describes the thrust and content of the successive chapters of the manuscript.

table of contents. A listing of a book's chapters and other sections (such as the front matter, appendix, bibliography, and index) with respective beginning page numbers in the order in which they appear.

terms. The financial conditions agreed to in a book contract.

tip sheet. An information sheet on a single book that presents general publication information (publication date, editor, ISBN, etc.), a brief synopsis of the book, information on competing titles, and other pertinent marketing data such as author profile and advance blurbs. The tip sheet is given to the sales and publicity departments.

title page. The page at the front of a book that lists the title, subtitle, author (and other contributors, such as translator or illustrator), as well as the publishing house and sometimes its logo.

trade books. Books distributed through the book trade—meaning bookstores and major book clubs—as opposed to, for example, mass-market paperbacks, which are often sold at magazine racks, newsstands, and supermarkets as well.

trade discount. The discount from the cover or list price that a publisher gives the bookseller. It is usually proportional to the number of books ordered (the larger the order, the greater the discount) and typically varies between 40 and 50 percent.

trade publisher. A publisher of books for a general readership—that is, nonprofessional, nonacademic books that are distributed primarily through bookstores.

unsolicited manuscript. A manuscript sent to an editor or agent without being requested.

vanity press. A publisher that prints books only at the author's expense—and will generally agree to publish virtually anything that is submitted and paid for. *See also* **self-publishing**; **subsidy publishing**.

word count. The number of words in a given document. When noted on a manuscript, the word count is usually rounded off to the nearest one hundred words.

work-for-hire. Writing done for an employer, or writing commissioned by a publisher or book packager who retains ownership of, and all rights pertaining to, the written material.

INDEX

BEYOND WORDS PUBLISHING, INC.

OUR CORPORATE MISSION
Inspire to Integrity

OUR DECLARED VALUES
We give to all of life as life has given us.
We honor all relationships.
Trust and stewardship are integral to fulfilling dreams.
Collaboration is essential to create miracles.
Creativity and aesthetics nourish the soul.
Unlimited thinking is fundamental.
Living your passion is vital.
Joy and humor open our hearts to growth.
It is important to remind ourselves of love.

To order or to request a catalog, contact
Beyond Words Publishing, Inc.
20827 N.W. Cornell Road, Suite 500
Hillsboro, OR 97124-9808
503-531-8700 or 1-800-284-9673

You can also visit our Web site at *www.beyondword.com*
or e-mail us at *info@beyondword.com*.